FRONTIER VIGILANTES

Volume 17

True Tales of the Old West

by

Charles L. Convis

Watercolor Cover by Mary Anne Convis

PIONEER PRESS, CARSON CITY, NEVADA

Library of Congress Catalog Card Number: 96-68502

ISBN 1-892156-07-5 (Volume)
ISBN 0-9651954-0-6 (Series)

Printed by
KNI, Incorporated
Anaheim, California

CONTENTS

ILLUSTRATIONS

A CALIFORNIA FIRST

The first vigilante execution in California — and the only one during Mexican rule — happened on April 7, 1837.

On March 28, Domingo Féliz, a poor ranchero of good reputation, had persuaded Manuel Requena, first alcalde of Los Angeles, to order Domingo's wife, Maria del Rosario Villa, to return home to her husband. Two years before, Maria had deserted Domingo for Gervasio Alipás, a scoundrel. She and her paramour, learning of the order, swore quick vengeance.

The next day, as Domingo rode out of town toward his rancho, Gervasio, with Maria's help, killed him. After the alcalde had a committee of citizens bring in the corpse, Gervasio and Maria were arrested and lodged in jail. The horror-struck town debated quick punishment for the murderers. Cooler heads prevailed, and the threatened summary executions were thwarted.

Popular clamor rose again on the 30th, after Domingo's funeral. The whole town talked about the assassination and the need to set an example to avoid further killings. But it was holy week, and the citizens didn't want to stain the remembrance of that solemn event with the blood of so foul an assassin as Gervasio. They fixed April 6, the first work day after Easter, as the day of execution.

A bad storm delayed the proceedings until April 7. Early that day the most respectable men in town met at the home of John Temple to organize the Junta Defensora de la Seguridad Publica (Board of Public Security). They elected Victor Prudon, French-born naturalized citizen of Mexico, president, and Manuel Arzaga, former secretary of the town council, secretary. Francisco Araujo, retired army officer, was appointed military commandant.

President Prudon, taking the chair, said the aims of the board were laudable and beneficial to the town, as well as necessary for future peace. The aims had their origins in the principles of natural law and self-preservation. Even the government, Prudon said, had to acknowledge the right of the people to form a superior tribunal with full power to give final sentence in all grave criminal cases. The need to preserve order showed that the board was a defender, not an offender.

Solemn speeches similar to Prudon's followed from the military commandant and others. Then the board unanimously adopted long resolutions embodying the same sentiments. Finally, the board decided that both Gervasio and Maria would be shot. The board would remain in permanent session until both murderers were dead.

In early afternoon, a sub-committee took copies of the resolutions to the alcalde. He convened the town council at two o'clock.

The Board of Public Security waited until three o'clock and then informed the alcalde the time for the town to act had expired. The board would carry out the resolutions itself.

Second Alcalde Abel Stearns, accompanied by a member of the town council, appeared before the board to ask if it recognized the lawful authority of the town. The board replied that it did.

"Then what is the significance of this unlawful assembly of armed men?" Stearns asked.

The board replied that the people had earnestly and repeatedly asked for the establishment in their territory of a superior tribunal with full power to investigate and punish all grave cases of crime. They added that the government had that duty, failing in the performance of which gave the people the right to take direct action. Stearns turned away, shaking his head.

At three-thirty the board took peaceable possession of the jail. At four both alcaldes arrived and presented the board with a town council resolution condemning their proposed action. The board shrugged them off.

The board asked Father Cabot of Mission San Fernando to attend for spiritual purposes. The father was unable to come in time, so the board decided the criminals would have to die without an opportunity to make their confessions.

Military Commandant Arraujo formed a firing squad. He issued the men rifles and gave them their orders.

At four-thirty Gervasio was brought forth and shot. Maria's execution followed. The Board of Public Security then dissolved and the people returned to their homes, satisfied they were secure from crime.

Colonel Mariano Chico reached California later that month to take office as governor. His first public act was to order the arrest of Prudon, Arzaga, and Araujo for their interference with the course of justice.

In June Chico went to Los Angeles to punish the three men. He heaped on them a tirade of abuse, containing all the vituperative epithets in his well-stocked vocabulary. The prisoners expected to be violently put to death. Araujo almost went insane from the apprehension. But Chico calmed down and pardoned all three.

Fifteen years would go by and sovereignty would pass from Mexico to the United States before California would have another vigilante execution.

Suggested reading: H. H. Bancroft, *Popular Tribunals, v.* 1 (San Francisco, The History Company, 1887).

PEACE IN SAN FRANCISCO

Sunday May 18, 1856, dawned serene and beautiful over San Francisco Bay. The sun glittered in a sky of azure crystals above the East Bay hills. Gentle breezes from the bay and ocean whispered peace, but the slap of hands on rifle stocks and the tramp of boots on cobblestones shouted war.

Three thousand men of the Second Committee of Vigilance marched to the San Francisco jail to take control of their city. A few deputy sheriffs and jailers, supported by a few more militiamen, tried to look brave as they stood their ground. But outnumbered one hundred to one, the only possible outcome was as clear as the sky overhead to the thousands of observers watching from Telegraph and Russian Hills and from the high bluffs between Montgomery and Sansome Streets to the southeast.

The trouble had come to a head four days before, when James King, editor of the *San Francisco Bulletin* published an editorial saying that James P. Casey, San Francisco Supervisor, had served time in New York's Sing Sing prison. Casey had admitted serving the prison time but he didn't think King should have put it in the newspaper. Within an hour after the editorial appeared, Casey stormed into King's office, screaming threats. King kicked him out.

An hour later as King was walking home, Casey, waiting in the street, shot him in the chest.

News of the attack traveled fast. San Francisco citizens felt outrage that a leading citizen had been shot down in the street in broad daylight.

A few months before, gambler Charles Cora had murdered the United States marshal after the marshal's wife and the gambler's prostitute girlfriend had an argument in a theater. The jury that tried Cora could not reach a verdict. Cries of "More hung men and less hung juries," came from frustrated citizens.

Five years before that, San Francisco citizens had organized a committee of vigilance to take control of their city. Now the streets were again filled with citizens, fed up with lawlessness, and shouts of "Hang him, hang him," rent the air.

Casey went directly to the police station and turned himself in to his friend, Sheriff David Scannell. Scannell spirited Casey away to the jail, where he thought he could keep the prisoner safe from the growing crowd.

During the next three days, the Second Committee of Vigilance was organized. Many of its leaders were veterans from the vigilantes of 1851. But this group looked more like a rebel army than a dissatisfied judicial tribunal. The men organized into companies of a hundred each, armed with rifles, and drilled in military precision. They even had a six-pound cannon.

When they reached the jail that Sunday morning, the vigilantes wheeled the cannon into position, aimed it at the jailhouse door, and demanded that Casey be turned over to them.

The day before, California Governor J. Neely Johnson had met with the vigilantes and privately told their leaders to do what they had to do and be quick about it. The governor had the support of the state militia, commanded by William Tecumseh Sherman, who would later become famous in the Civil War. But many militiamen were sympathetic to the vigilantes. Some of them switched sides, and Sherman resigned rather than fight against his own men.

Sheriff Scannell, looking at the horde of angry citizens, released Casey to the vigilantes. They marched their prisoner to their Fort Vigilance headquarters on Sacramento Street and began plans for the trial.

Then someone remembered the gambler, Charles Cora. He was also demanded and delivered up by the sheriff. The two trials were held on the same day, Cora's in the afternoon and Casey's in the evening.

Shortly after Cora's trial started, news came that King had died. The rest of the day's proceedings grew even more grim.

The trials bore some resemblance to regular court proceedings. The defendants were allowed to question the witnesses against them and to present evidence of their own. They were even allowed attorneys, provided the attorneys were members of the Vigilance Committee.

The jury returned verdicts of guilty and sentenced each man to hang. Yard arms were rigged up on the roof of Fort Vigilance. The hangings were set for May 22, the day of King's funeral.

When that day arrived, the gathered crowd filled Portsmouth Square and watched in eager anticipation. The two prisoners were marched out, and the guttural roar of citizens rose into the air. Casey screamed as the hood was lowered over his head. The men were hanged together.

A certain kind of peace returned to the streets of San Francisco as the two bodies continued hanging from Fort Vigilance, and the church bells tolled for James King. Two months passed before another San Francisco citizen was murdered.

Suggested reading: Stanton A. Coblentz, *Villains and Vigilantes* (New York: Thomas Yoseloff, Inc., 1936).

FOUND GUILTY! TURN HIM LOOSE

In June, 1856, San Francisco's Second Committee of Vigilance tried David Smith Terry for assault with intent to kill. One month before, the committee had executed gambler Charles Cora and ex-convict and city supervisor James P. Casey. But Terry was a justice on the California Supreme Court!

Sterling A. Hopkins had been the hangman for the Cora and Casey executions. The executive committee of the vigilantes ordered him to arrest Rube Maloney. Maloney was a member of the Law and Order group, opposed to the vigilantes.

Hopkins tried to arrest Maloney on June 21, while Terry and other Law and Order men were guarding him. As Hopkins and Terry struggled for a pistol, Terry drew his Bowie knife and stabbed Hopkins in the throat.

Shortly after the stabbing, Terry took refuge in the Law and Order armory. But with sixteen men on the inside and a howling mob of a thousand outside, he surrendered to the vigilantes to avoid further bloodshed.

Terry knew that if Hopkins died, he would surely be executed. Yet he wrote his wife that he faced his vigilante trial unafraid. He said he had sworn to uphold the constitutions of the state and the nation, and he would not allow Maloney, or any person, to be arrested by ruffians, working outside the law.

A federal officer, arrested with Terry, accepted "parole" with the agreement that he would not criticize the vigilantes. Not Terry! As he prepared for his trial, he denounced the vigilantes as a "powerful organization of men acting in open and armed rebellion against the lawful authorities of this state."

Terry's trial began on June 27, while Hopkins still hovered between life and death. Terry was allowed to select one of the vigilantes as his attorney.

Terry claimed to have acted in self defense. He said he had heard a pistol discharge and he saw the federal officer staggering as though hit. He thought he would be the next target, so he drew his knife and stabbed Hopkins.

As the trial progressed, some newspapers called Terry a human-beast who slaked his thirst on the blood of others. The state governor worked behind the scenes, attempting to get the supreme court justice released. There were rumors that the vigilantes would release Terry if both he and the chief justice resigned from the court. Terry refused to consider it. He said, "If I leave this building alive, I'll leave it as a justice of the Supreme Court of this state."

The trial ended on July 22. Swift medical attention in repairing severed arteries had saved Hopkins' life. In fact, Hopkins appeared before the vigilantes during the trial, requesting that he be allowed to resolve the case by a financial arrangement with the accused. The fact that Hopkins survived encouraged Terry and his Law and Order supporters. No longer did it appear that the vigilantes would hang a supreme court justice. However, another ominous development soon occurred.

On July 29 the vigilantes hanged two men just outside the Fort Vigilance headquarters, where Terry was being held prisoner. One of the men, Joseph Hetherington, had killed a doctor five days earlier. Arrested by the police, he was taken from them by vigilantes, demanding quick justice. The other man, Philander Brace, was tried at the same time as Hetherington, but for an older murder. The two men were hanged on a hastily-built scaffold. As the executioner approached him, Brace yelled out that he wanted to be hung between Hetherington and Terry, like Christ between the two thieves.

After the vigilantes executed Hetherington and Brace, they had great difficulty deciding what to do with Terry. The full Committee of Vigilance wanted to find him guilty and banish him from California upon penalty of death if he ever returned. The executive committee wanted to find him guilty and remove him from the supreme court. But the outlaw organization had no way to enforce either decision.

Finally, on August 7, the executive committee prevailed. They announced that Terry had been found guilty and should be removed from the supreme court. They turned him loose the same day.

Vigilantes in the street, disappointed that they could not watch another hanging, howled for Terry's life. With the help of friends and the cooperation of some of the vigilantes, themselves, he got to a United States naval vessel in the harbor. From there he made it safely to his Stockton home.

Terry continued serving on the Supreme Court. Three years later he killed a United States senator in a famous duel. Terry was later killed by a United States marshal, who was protecting Stephen J. Field, a United States Supreme Court Justice, from Terry.

Suggested reading: A. R. Buchanan, *David S. Terry of California, Dueling Judge* (San Marino: Huntington Library, 1956).

INDEPENDENCE DAY IN DOWNIEVILLE

Juanita, barely twenty, loved her husband, Jose. As in most California mining camps, the gringos had driven the Mexicans out, so Jose became a gambler in nearby Downieville. Juanita would often stand by her beloved as he worked the green-clothed tables.

Miners, hungering for the sight of a decent woman, liked to look at the tiny, dark-haired beauty with such soft olive skin and lustrous eyes. One miner once walked forty miles just to see a woman. Another charged five dollars admission to his wedding and sold enough tickets to finance his honeymoon. In that woman-starved community Juanita was noticed and talked about.

On July 4, 1851, Jack Cannon from Australia, like thousands of other miners, celebrated American Independence Day. John B. Weller, candidate for Congress, was Downieville's orator for the day. He spoke eloquently of liberty and freedom:

"The United States, the youngest country in the world, is the most free," Weller proclaimed. "Not yet a year old, California is the greatest state in our great union. And who made it great? You miners."

Drunken roars of approval reverberated through the town. Cannon, imagining by then that he could have fought with Washington at Valley Forge, jumped on a horse and rode into Craycroft's saloon so Juanita could admire him.

But she wasn't there. So Cannon and Lawson, his partner, went to her house.

Cannon knocked at Juanita's door.

"Who is there, Señor?" Her voice shook with terror.

"Jack Cannon. Let me in."

"My husband is not here, Señor."

Cannon kicked the door down and lurched inside. Juanita backed against the wall and faced the man, her face whitened, his breath reeking with liquor. He moved closer, trying to bury his face in her thick, beautiful hair.

"Leave her alone and come out of there," shouted Lawson. He pulled Cannon out and apologized to Juanita. "I'm very sorry Señora."

"Too damn stuck up for a greaser," Cannon slurred. "Ought to be proud that a white man would even speak to her."

Juanita trembled as she looked at the shattered door. Would he come back, or would others come? The streets were overrun with drunken miners. Would this ugly day of American celebration ever end? Never had she so clearly realized the high cost of being a woman.

When Jose came home she sobbed in his arms, telling him of the day's horror. He soothed her and repaired the door.

Cannon came back the next morning. Later, Lawson would say his friend had sobered up and came to pay for the damage. Juanita was making *tortillas* when Cannon arrived, and she seized a knife. Jose stood at the door, blocking Cannon's entry.

Cannon spoke in mixed English and Spanish. A passer-by thought he heard something about a whore. Perhaps it was about a door. The Spanish words, *puta* and *puerta,* also are close. But Juanita heard it like the passer-by. She plunged her knife into Cannon's chest.

Word spread quickly up and down the Yuba River.

"A greaser woman killed Jack Cannon!"

Cannon was a camp favorite. The soul of honor, he would not normally harm a fly. His thoughts were simple, with nothing of cheating or chicanery. He was enormously popular; the kind of man who could have come back, sober and remorseful, to pay up.

Enraged miners had locked Jose up, and Juanita was now alone. Cries of "hang her," echoed up and down the crowd-filled streets.

Cooler persons talked about a trial. They would use the speaker's platform, still standing on the lower plaza after the earlier festivities had ended.

"Yes, a trial," someone shouted. "To show the American spirit. We'll give her a trial and then hang her!"

Twelve quickly volunteered to be jurors. John Rose of Rose's Bar was proclaimed the judge. William Speare shouted, "Let me prosecute the hussy."

Then a Nevada lawyer, C. C. Fair who had been campaigning for Weller, mounted a whiskey barrel. "I'll defend the girl," he shouted. "We can't let mob rule — "

A dozen men kicked the barrel away and Fair, bloody and bruised, fled for his life. Later, his death at the hands of a paramour would lead to one of California's most famous murder trials.

Someone asked Weller if he'd defend. But the great Fourth of July orator, who would one day be California's governor, let common sense override chivalry.

Then another Nevada lawyer named Thayer, volunteered.

"In the name of your mothers, sisters, wives, sweethearts," he pleaded, "I beg you not to shed this woman's blood. As Christians — "

"To hell with Christians!" someone shouted.

Thayer was knocked from the platform and kicked down a gauntlet until he was out of town. Downieville had no time for such nonsense. A good man lay slain, and justice had to be served!

With another supply of whiskey to fortify them, the jury returned the

JUANITA
California State Library

expected verdict: hanged on the bridge at four o'clock.

There was little Juanita could do. She was not allowed to see Jose. He had been taken, battered and bleeding, into the hills. She sent her few personal things to other Mexican women. There were less than a dozen in the area. She played her guitar and waited. She did wonder what had become of her one gringo friend.

Dr. Cyrus D. Aiken had come directly from college to Downieville, where he hung up his shingle to practice medicine. He had treated Juanita like a lady. He pleaded with the judge and the jury foreman:

"I tell you, it is true," he said. "You won't be kiling one, but two. Juanita is going to have a baby."

"We ain't greenhorns, doc," the miners jeered. They sent him the way of Fair and Thayer.

A thousand miners, now silent and somber, escorted Juanita to the bridge, where another two thousand waited. A plank had been rigged out over the river, and a rope with a noose at its end hung down from above. Two men, axes on their shoulders, stood beside the ropes that held up the plank.

Juanita, wearing her best black dress, took the noose as it was handed to her. Her deep gray eyes grew black and challenged the crowd. She stared at them with a sudden blaze of defiance which turned slowly to contempt.

The crowd included some who would later be famous. Stage driver, Hank Monk, said, "I never seen a woman show grit like that."

Stephen J. Field, later a Justice of the United States Supreme Court, voiced no protest. Neither did Charles Felton nor William Stewart, both to become United States Senators from Nevada.

When her guards asked if she had any last words, Juanita replied softly, "I would do it again. The man insulted me."

Juanita herself adjusted the noose about her throat. She smoothed her blue-black hair down over the coarse rope. Her face was calm and her hands steady as she pushed back her long braids.

"Adios, señores," she said softly to the guards.

She nodded her head, the axes swung, and the plank dropped. Juanita's body, like a ghastly top, twisted round and round for a half hour while three thousand watched on that Independence Day celebration.

Suggested reading: Mrs. Fremont Older, *Love Stories of Old California* (New York: Coward-McCann, Inc., 1940).

STEP OUTSIDE FOR A MINUTE

Wyoming vigilantes were first organized in Cheyenne in January, 1868. About two hundred men formed the initial gunny sack brigade. They usually wore soldier's overcoats — not hard to get in those days — with burlap sacks, containing eye holes, drawn down over their heads. They worked quietly. If they thought someone should leave town permanently, a small delegation would advise the man that his health would be improved by a long trip.

If a man so warned was too stubborn to comply, someone would tap him on the shoulder in a saloon, saying, "Say, pard, there's a gentleman outside that would like to speak with you for a minute." When the man stepped outside he would meet several dozen masked men summoning, "Come with us."

No explanations or promises availed at that stage of the proceedings. The work was done quickly and efficiently, and another unwelcome member of the community would be found dangling from a telegraph pole or upraised wagon tongue. Trees were scarce in much of inhabited Wyoming.

Charles Martin was one of the vigilantes' first victims. He had left a young wife and baby boy in Missouri to go to Cheyenne. Soon after his arrival, he and a man named Jones were accused of a $5000 robbery. But no proof being available, no charges were filed.

Then Martin and Jones built the Beauvis Hall, and citizens wondered where the money came from. The partners argued and Martin killed Jones. He was charged with murder.

The jury acquitted, but W. W. Corlett had testified for the prosecution, and Martin swore to get even. As soon as he was released, Martin rented a livery team, bought a plug hat, and took two women for a drive around town. A friend — later the city marshal — warned Martin to be careful or he would get into trouble. But later that day Martin said, "By God, I'll have Corlett for breakfast."

That night in a dance hall someone tapped Martin on the shoulder and asked him to step outside for a minute. In spite of Martin's explanations and promises to leave town, the gunny sack brigade marched him to Capitol and 16th Streets and hanged him.

Corlett heard nothing about the threats or the hanging until the next day, but he displayed no grief over the affair.

Suggested reading: C. G. Coutant, "History of Wyoming," in *Annals of Wyoming*, v. 13, no. 2 (April, 1941).

TREACHERY AND DEFIANCE

In the 1850s Bill Thorington farmed at the forks of the Carson River, near present Gardnerville, Nevada. The imposing man — over six feet tall and two hundred pounds — had won his nickname, Lucky, in 1853 when he arrived in the Carson Valley and introduced its residents and passing emigrants to his thimblerig or shell game. Lucky Bill never lost.

Bill's wife and twelve-year-old son, Jerome, joined him in 1854. He prospered by operating a toll road and a trading post, in addition to his farm.

In spring 1858 Lucky Bill had his eyes on some cattle that Frenchman Henry Gordier was pasturing along the Truckee River to the north. Bill's friend, William Edwards, who had arrived from Merced County, California, after murdering a man there, also wanted the cattle and had tried unsuccessfully to buy the Frenchman out.

"Why don't we just kill him and divide the cattle," Lucky Bill suggested.

Edwards agreed, and he shot Gordier in the back. He and Lucky Bill buried the body, made a forged bill of sale from the Frenchman to Edwards, and divided up the herd.

But the Frenchman's friends in nearby Honey Lake, California, found the body, and formed a vigilance committee to look into why the cattle had suddenly augmented the herds of Lucky Bill and Edwards.

Eventually the vigilantes found an Asa Snow, whom they suspected had knowledge of the crime, having moved into Gordier's cabin after the man had disappeared. Snow denied knowing anything about it, so the vigilantes decided a little hanging might refresh his memory.

Snow, abusive and defiant, insisted he was innocent and dared the committee to hang him. They strung him up on a pine tree, let him hang a while, then lowered him for more questions. Snow still insisted that he knew nothing, and continued to defy and curse the vigilantes.

A second "hanging" produced the same result. But when the vigilantes pulled Snow up the third time, they had let him hang too long. He was beyond questioning when they lowered him to the ground.

Edwards had escaped, but the committee arrested Lucky Bill. They organized a tribunal and conducted a trial in a barn near Carson City, while they were building the gallows just outside.

A few spectators, friendly to Lucky Bill, were allowed inside the barn to watch. The judge, jurors, and other spectators were all armed to the teeth. The evidence against Lucky Bill was slight, but he had been living openly with Martha Lamb while he was married to Maria, Jerome's mother.

The Mormons had been recalled to Zion the year before to prepare their defenses against the United States Army, and the vigilantes wanted to eliminate all traces of plural marriage or similar relationships from the Carson valley. They sentenced Lucky Bill, who was not a Mormon, to death.

But the committee still wanted Edwards, and they thought up a way to find him. By then, Jerome Thorington was a bright, honest, sixteen-year-old lad, unaware that his father might be a murderer. Certain that Jerome would know where his father's friend was hiding, the vigilantes made an offer to the boy that they said would save his father's life. If the boy brought Edwards to them, his father would go free.

It would be dangerous, Jerome knew that. Edwards was a powerful, well-armed, desperate man. Just finding his hideout was not enough for the vigilantes, as they feared to attack him there. They wanted the boy to bring Edwards to a cabin that Lucky Bill sometimes used. The vigilantes would be hiding inside.

Willing to do almost anything to save his father, whom he thought innocent, the boy set out for where he was sure Edwards would be, a secluded canyon in the Carson Range, southwest of Genoa.

Edwards did not know that Lucky Bill had been caught. Jerome told him his father wanted Edwards to come to the cabin so they could plan together how to avoid arrest. Edwards, suspicious, refused at first.

"We can stay hid out better if we keep apart," Edwards insisted.

But with the burden of his father's life on him, the boy continued to reason and plead, assuring Edwards that no harm would come to him. Finally Edwards agreed.

"But if this is a trick," he warned the boy, "you're as good as dead, you know."

Edwards followed the boy through the woods, clutching his revolver in one hand, his rifle in the other. Long after midnight they reached Lucky Bill's cabin. Edwards didn't suspect the cabin's darkness; obviously his crime partner woudn't have a light in the window.

When Jerome reached the door, Edwards grabbed his shoulder and pulled him back. Then he listened for a long time, his ear pressed to the door. Finally he opened the door and stepped inside.

A gun crashed down on Edwards' head. When he came to he was

bound hand and foot, looking up at a circle of armed vigilantes, their menacing faces barely visible in the near darkness.

The vigilante tribunal tried Edwards, convicted him, and sentenced him to death about as quickly as they had Lucky Bill.

Then came the question of the vigilantes' promise to Jerome Thorington. Some of the men thought the promise should be honored. They took a vote, and honor lost.

Lucky Bill faced his hanging with more courage than was shown by his executioners. They had drawn straws to see who would drive the wagon out from under the rudely-built gallows. Secretly marking the shortest straw, they tricked Lawrence Frey, a young boy, into driving the team.

On June 19, 1858, the vigilantes boosted Lucky Bill into the wagon and adjusted the noose around his neck. Staring defiantly at the men around him, the condemned man began singing his favorite song, *The Last Rose of Summer*. The executioners jumped out of the wagon and nodded for the Frey boy, holding the reins, to drive the team forward.

But young Frey started crying and refused to slap the reins down on the rumps of the horses. Angry vigilantes began flashing knives toward the wagon and its occupants, an unwilling boy in tears and a prisoner, singing his defiance.

Lucky Bill stopped his singing to yell at the men on the ground, "I never lived like a hog and I ain't gonna be butchered like one, now."

Turning to young Frey, he added, "Don't worry, boy. I'll take care of it."

With that he jumped out of the wagon to a strangling death.

One wonders what went through sixteen-year-old Jerome's mind when he realized what the vigilantes had done to him, as well as to his father.

Jerome drank himself to death within a few years. His mother's mind snapped and she spent the last forty years of her life in asylums.

Suggested reading: Hubert Howe Bancroft, *Popular Tribunals*, v. 1 (San Francisco: The History Company, 1887).

16

HANGED AS A GENERAL NUISANCE

When the wagon train left Colorado in early 1863 for the gold fields of Virginia City and Bannack in Idaho Territory (present Montana) two men vied for captain. One of them, Jack Slade, had grown up in Illinois in a town founded by his father. His father had become United States marshal for Illinois, a state legislator, and a member of the United States Congress. Slade had become a fearless stage line superintendent, famous for executing robbers and horse thieves without bothering about arrests or trials. But drinking got the best of him and he degenerated into a depraved killer.

Slade did have a kind side. Once, when his men shot up a rustler's hangout, they orphaned a small boy, whom Slade adopted and treated as his own son. Slade was heading north with his mistress, Virginia Dale, because too many men hated him in Colorado and Wyoming.

The other contender for wagon train captain was James Williamson, who had grown up in southwestern Pennsylvania and come to Colorado in the gold rush. He had decided to move on to the new discoveries in the north.

Williamson was elected captain, but he had no hard feelings for Slade, appointing him his lieutenant. Williamson said, "I never had a man with me that I got along with better." Slade also respected Williamson, and they had no trouble on the train.

Williamson received the honorary title of "Cap" for his valiant leadership of the wagon train in resisting Indian attacks.

Both men started ranches near Virginia City. Slade did a little freighting on the side, and Williamson ran a pack train over the Bitter Root Mountains into Elk City, Idaho.

By fall 1863, organized outlaws were riding roughshod over the miners, ranchers, and businessmen in the area. The outlaws' leader, Henry Plummer, had got himself elected sheriff of both Virginia City and Bannack so he could learn which stages and travelers had money and could then cover for his men when they robbed and killed. Plummer had killed at least two men and had served prison time in California before he moved north.

Cap Williamson led a posse in December, 1863, that captured George Ives, the first of Plummer's gang of road agents and killers to be executed. With no formal law in the unorganized territory, the posse and local citizens elected the judge, the prosecutor, the defense counsel for Ives, and the jurors.

After he was found guilty and ordered hanged immediately, Ives asked for a short delay so he could write his mother and sisters back in Wisconsin and make his will. He had come from a prominent family that knew nothing of his criminal behavior.

Colonel Wilbur Sanders, who had served as prosecutor and would later have a distinguished career, including service as a United States Senator, listened carefully to Ives.

"Sanders," a man called out, "ask him how much time he gave the Dutchman." The Dutchman was one of at least two recent victims whom Ives had killed in cold blood.

Two days after Ives' execution, Sanders and about two dozen others, many of them leading citizens in the community, organized a committee of vigilance. They took the vigilante oath to "arrest thieves and murderers, pledging their sacred honor to violate no laws of right or their standard of justice." Williamson signed the oath first and was named the executive officer of the group.

In less than six weeks the vigilance committee had broken the intrenched power of Plummer's gang, hanging twenty-one men. Four more men had been ordered banished, and others on the list had disappeared voluntarily. The men on the committee had kept their mutual promises that vigilante justice would be swift, sure, and permanent.

Slade was never suspected of being in Plummer's gang. In fact, he claimed to be a vigilante, but there was no proof, and it seems unlikely. Slade was just a drunken nuisance.

He would often get drunk in a Virginia City hotel and tear up the furniture in his room. He always paid the damage after sobering up, but the businessmen were tired of his drunken brawls, shooting up saloons, threatening citizens, and destruction of property. They asked the vigilantes to do something.

No one knows why this organization which included so many of Montana's respected citizens decided to take action against a man who had never been a robber or killer in their area. But on March 10, 1864, James Williamson led a group of men that picked Slade up.

Slade begged for his life, but all they gave him was a few minutes to write a note to Virginia Dale. By the time she got there, Slade was slowly twisting at the end of a rope fastened to a corral gate in a slaughter pen behind a Virginia City store.

Suggested reading: Hoffman Birney, *Vigilantes* (New York: Penn Publishing Co., 1929).

TOTAL DESTRUCTION

Red Yager and G. W. Brown, hanged on New Year's Day, 1864, were the first victims of the Montana Vigilance Committee, which had been formed nine days earlier. They confessed and provided more names of gang members. The committee, neither a law-enforcement body nor a judicial one, acted like a military force, determined to seek out and kill the enemy.

Henry Plummer and two others were next. The vigilantes hanged them on January 10, using a gallows which Plummer, as sheriff, had used in legal executions of criminals.

Plummer had fled California, and he became sheriff at Bannack and Virginia City as a cover for his gang of cut-throats. The mastermind behind every robbery and killing by the gang, he had led every sheriff's posse on its unsuccessful pursuit of his own henchmen.

But, as might be expected, vigilante justice sometimes left doubts. A good example was the execution on January 11 of Frank Pizanthia.

A Mexican, Pizanthia lived in a little cabin against a hillside, overlooking Bannack. No one knew much about him, except that someone had identified him as a member of Plummer's gang. The only Mexican in the camp, he was usually called Greaser Joe. He, alone, fought back when the vigilantes came.

George Copley and Smith Ball, two esteemed citizens, led the vigilantes to Pizanthia's cabin. They marched to the door, and Copley called out, "Come on, you greaser, we're here to hang you."

Hearing no answer, they stepped inside, ignoring the advice of comrades who warned them to take care. Pizanthia's rifle roared, and Copley fell, a bullet in his heart. Then Pizanthia shot Ball in the hip. The rage of the assembled vigilantes now knew no bounds.

For the moment, the attackers fell back, fearing more shots from the lone rifle in the cabin. Then someone remembered that a mountain howitzer had been left in the camp by a wagon train. Men with military experience ran to get the gun.

They set the howitzer up on a box, loaded it, and fired. But they forgot to cut the fuse, and the ball passed through the cabin without exploding. After the second round left two more holes in the cabin, the men realized that they were too close to safely cut fuses short enough.

"We need to back up if we want to blow him out of there," someone shouted.

"Hell, he's probably hiding in the chimney," another offered. "Let's stay here and blast it apart."

The third shot almost demolished the cabin. A storming party rushed in and found Pizanthia under the rubble, alive but badly injured. They dragged their prey out, while others took down a clothes line. They fastened the line around Pizanthia's neck.

Simon Estes climbed a nearby pole and wound the clothes line around the top, while others hoisted the twisting, squirming Pizanthia as high as they could. When Estes had the rope securely fastened, the men below let Pizanthia drop. The crowd then discharged more than a hundred pistol shots into Pizanthia's swaying, choking body.

"Hey, boys," shouted Estes, "stop your shooting a minute so's I can come down."

While some of the crowd satiated their blood thirst, others tore down the rest of the cabin, piled the debris together, and set it on fire.

"Let's drag the son of a bitch into the woods and leave his body for the wolves," someone suggested.

"No, let's burn the greaser right here while we got the fire," another shouted, exultantly. Others yelled their agreement.

They took down Pizanthia's riddled body and threw it on the funeral pyre. Some accounts claim that Pizanthia was thrown on the fire alive and shot afterward.

"Look at him cook in his own grease," someone shouted, laughing.

The destruction was complete. Not a vestige of the poor wretch, not even the trace of a bone, remained when the fire had burned out. It was a ghastly end for a determined man.

The next morning several prostitutes from the camp came to pan the still-smoldering ashes, hoping to find gold from Pizanthia's reputed hoard or from his teeth.

Suggested reading: Thomas J. Dimsdale, *The Vigilantes of Montana* (Norman: University of Oklahoma, 1953).

FIVE AT ONE TIME

While the Bannack vigilantes were executing gang leader Henry Plummer and two of his men plus Frank Pizanthia — apparently not a member — Virginia City vigilantes were also busy. On the evening of January 13, 1864, two nights after Pizanthia's execution, five hundred armed men quietly surrounded Virginia City. In spite of their efforts, they learned later that one man — Bill Hunter — had escaped. But they captured five of Plummer's men.

Frank Parish, arrested quietly in a store, was the first brought before the vigilance committee the next day.

"What am I arrested for?" he asked.

"For being a road-agent, thief, and accessory to many murders and robberies."

"I am innocent."

But after Parish learned what the committee knew, he confessed to more crimes than they had charged him with. The committee turned him over to a guard, as Clubfoot George Lane was brought in. He, too, had been arrested quietly in a store. About two years before, Lane had escaped from Idaho vigilantes by surrendering to Federal authorities and leaving the territory.

"Why am I arrested?" Lane asked.

When he heard the same answer Parish did, he replied, "If you hang me, you will hang an innocent man." He asked to have a minister pray for him. One was brought, and Lane spent the remainder of his hours attending to his own soul.

Boone Helm, the most dangerous of the lot, was brought in next. He had been arrested in front of a hotel when three armed men slipped up on him, one on each side, and the third held a pistol at the back of his head. Helm had killed about a dozen men in Missouri, California, Idaho, and Montana. He had spent the hard 1858-1859 winter in Idaho with five companions. Helm, resorting to cannibalism, was the only survivor.

"If I'd known you wanted me, you'd have had a hell of a time taking me," he announced to the committee. "It's a good thing you had three of them sneaking up on me."

The committee announced the charges.

"I'm as innocent as a babe unborn," Helm said. "I'll swear to it on a bible."

They handed him a bible. He took the oath, invoking the most terrible penalties on his soul if he wasn't truthful. He kissed the bible when he finished. His sacrilege appalled the committee.

"Do you want to see a minister?"

"Hell, no. I'm not afraid to die. Bring me some whiskey."

Jack Gallagher was brought in next. Laughing and swearing, at first he thought the investigation a joke.

"You're charged with murder and sentenced to hang," the committee announced.

Gallagher began to cry. "My God!" he said, "must I die that way?"

He was dragged, swearing, out of the room.

Hayes Lyons was the last one brought in. Seven months before, he and Gallagher, with others, had killed John Dillingham, Plummer's only honest deputy sheriff. Friends had warned Lyons to get out of town, but he didn't want to leave his mistress. Like the others, he initially claimed innocence.

After Lyons' examination ended, the committee sent fifteen men out to arrest two more persons, reported as suspicious. These men were brought in, but when no evidence appeared, they were released.

By the time the vigilantes marched their five prisoners into the street, a crowd of seven or eight thousand persons had gathered. They came from all parts of Alder Gulch to witness the executions.

Paris Pfouts, Vigilance Committee president, asked if any of the prisoners wanted to confess in public and give information about crimes of others. None spoke up.

Then Jack Gallagher shouted, "I will not be hung in public." He drew his pocket-knife. "I'll cut my throat first."

A vigilante drew his pistol. "One more move like that and I'll shoot you down like a dog, "the determined man said.

Gallagher cursed as they tied his arms.

"Don't make a fool of yourself, Jack," Helm said. "There's no sense in being afraid to die."

Armed vigilantes formed a hollow square around the prisoners and began a slow and solemn march toward an uncompleted building which had its walls up but no roof. Other armed men moved into the crowd to prevent any rescue attempt. The procession halted for a time, waiting for ropes to be suspended from the building's crossbeam.

Lane called out to Judge Dance, a man he knew. "Can't you say a good word for me," Lane pleaded.

"It would be no use, George. Your dealings with me have always been honorable, but the evidence is very strong against you."

"Well, then, will you pray with me?"

"Of course."

The judge, Lane, and Gallagher all dropped to their knees and prayed fervently.

"For God's sake," shouted Helm. "if you're going to hang me, get it done. If you're not, I want a bandage on my finger."

While the three men were praying, Lyons asked someone to remove his hat for him.

"I want to show my respect." Lyon said.

Parish seemed contrite, but Helm continued to laugh and swear.

Gallagher spoke to someone he recognized in the crowd. "Say, old fellow, I'm going to heaven. I'll be there in time to open the gate for you."

With the noosed ropes in place, five dry-goods boxes were positioned below, each with a jerk-rope attached. The guards made their prisoners step up on the boxes.

Clubfoot George Lane took the box at the east end. Then followed Hayes Lyons, Jack Gallagher, Boone Helm, and, near the west wall, Frank Parish.

Paris Pfouts stepped forward. "If you have any dying requests to make, this is your last chance," he said.

"How do I look, boys?" leered Gallagher, "with a halter around my neck."

"Your time is short," Pfouts repeated. "We'll listen to your requests."

"I want another drink of whiskey," Gallagher said.

Some of the crowd seemed surprised, others disappointed.

An old miner spoke up. "We told 'em that we'd do what they asked. Give him the liquor."

Someone brought a tumblerfull. They had to slacken the rope so Gallagher could throw his head back far enough to drink.

"I hope Almighty God curses every one of you," Gallagher sputtered. "And I hope I meet all of you in the lowest pit of hell."

The committee had decided to do the executions one at a time. Clubfoot George was first. Just as the men reached down for the ropes to pull the box out, he saw someone he recognized in the crowd. "Good-bye, old fellow, I'm gone," he shouted. Without waiting for the box to be jerked away, he leaped forward and died quickly.

"There goes one to hell," muttered Boone Helm.

Jack Gallagher was next. His last words — "I hope that forked lightning strikes every strangling villain of" — were interrupted when his box was jerked out.

"Kick away, old fellow," said Boone Helm, calmly watching from the next box as Gallagher strangled. "My turn comes next. I'll be in hell with you in a minute." Then he shouted to the crowd: "Every man for his principles! Hurrah for Jeff Davis! Let her rip!"

His falling body snapped the rope with a loud twang, and he died instantly of a broken neck.

Frank Parish had requested that his kerchief be draped like a veil over his face. He was silent as he dropped.

Hayes Lyons, looking at the swaying companions on each side , made incessant pleas — that his mistress could have his body, that her watch be returned to her, that he not be left hanging an unseemly time. He died without a struggle.

The bodies hung for two hours and then were cut down by friends, who buried the men on Cemetery Hill. John X. Beidler, later a deputy United States marshal, was the official adjuster of ropes at the hangings. Some time later, when Beidler was talking about the executions, a man, obviously sympathetic to the victims, asked:

"Now, when you come to hang that fellow, didn't you sympathize with him — didn't you feel for him?"

"Sure I did," Beidler replied, "I felt for his left ear."

George Lane's clubfoot, in the sock he wore at the execution, was later dug up to prove the location of the graves. It is on view in a Virginia City museum. Some say Jack Gallagher's head was obtained after the burial, and the skull, after being boiled clean, is used today in the rites of a secret fraternal organization.

Bill Hunter, the desperado who had escaped, was captured by the vigilantes in the Gallatin Valley on February 3. They took him to a nearby tree, but they had no way to build a drop. They threw a rope over a limb and hoisted the man into eternity. In his final contortions, while certainly unconscious, Hunter freed one arm and went through the pantomine of drawing a pistol and cocking and shooting it six times.

During a six-week period that winter, Montana vigilantes hanged almost two dozen men.

Suggested reading: Nathaniel P. Langford, *Vigilante Days and Ways* (Bozeman: Montana State University, 1957).

HOME-MADE JUSTICE FOR A FRIEND

When congress created Idaho Territory in March, 1863, it failed to enact a penal code. It may have thought the existing laws stayed in force, ignoring the fact that Idaho was made up of parts of four different territories. Inconsistencies between the parts would make a uniform law impossible. So the territory had no law until its first legislature met in December, 1863. Hill Beachy, proprietor of the Luna House, Lewiston's main hotel, shows how the people took care of the nine-month hiatus.

Beachy, a Missourian, had gone to California in the gold rush and then moved north to Lewiston. After packing, government contracting, and managing a stage line, he had become a hotelman.

Beachy's closest friend was Lloyd Magruder, a wealthy merchant who ran a sixty-mule pack train from Lewiston into the mines of present Montana. In September, 1863, Magruder packed the three hundred miles into Virginia City.

The night before Magruder left, Beachy dreamed that his friend was killed by a man who crept up behind him with an axe. He related the dream to his wife, Maggie, and she wanted him to warn Magruder. Thinking about Magruder's heavy investment, the facts that he was leaving that morning, and a warning would probably be ignored, Beachy declined. He thought a warning might worry his friend, and he didn't want to do that.

When Magruder reached the crest of the Bitter Root Mountains he met three men — Chris Lowry, Doc Howard, and Jim Romaine — whom he had seen earlier in Lewiston. He let them travel with him and they helped care for the mules.

Beachy, remembering his dream, was relieved to learn six weeks later that Magruder had reached the Bannack and Virginia City mines safely.

In October Magruder had sold all his goods for twenty-four thousand dollars in gold dust, and he headed back to Lewiston. He hired the same three men who had traveled with him before, plus William Page, a trapper, to help with the train. He also allowed four other men to travel with him, Charley Allen, two young brothers, Horace and Robert Chalmers, and Bill Phillips. All of these were carrying gold dust from their prospecting.

HILL BEACHY

Idaho State Historical Society

Learning that a pack train was leaving the mines for Lewiston three days ahead of him, Magruder sent a message to his wife that he would be leaving with a strongly guarded train in twelve days. He did this because reaching Lewiston a week or so before he was expected might fool any robbers who planned to hold him up on his return trip. Gold dust was a more attractive target for robbers than miners' supplies.

The return trip was uneventful until the train reached the Bitter Root Mountains, about halfway to Lewiston. There they camped just east of Lolo Pass on a high ridge above a perpendicular cliff, looming several hundred feet above a gorge.

That evening, with snow falling heavily, Magruder, Lowry, Howard, and Romaine were at the campfire, the others in their blankets. Suddenly Lowry slipped up on Magruder, who was lighting his pipe at the fire, and split his skull with an axe.

Bill Phillips jumped to his feet, cursing , and Romaine stabbed him with a Bowie knife. Howard grabbed the axe from Lowry, jumped over Magruder's body, and killed both Chalmers brothers as they lay in their blanets. Charley Allen rose up, wondering what had awakened him. Howard dropped the axe, grabbed Magruder's double-barrelled shotgun, and fired both barrels into Allen's head from a six-inch distance.

Throughout the killing orgy, Page cowered in his blankets. He had been told what would happen and warned that if he objected, he would also be killed. The killers divided the gold of the victims among themselves, with a share to Page.

From Page's later confession, after turning state's evidence, it was learned that Lowry, Howard, and Romaine had originally planned to kill Magruder on the earlier trip, but found no opportunity then.

After the murders, the victims were thrown into the gorge. The train of mules, except for four saddle mounts and one pack animal for the killers and Page, were also killed, and the pack equipment burned. Howard selected Magruder's favorite mount for himself

A two-foot snowfall after the massacre covered almost all signs of the gory slaughter.

The killers had hoped to avoid Lewiston, but deep snow brought them close to starving and they were forced to stop there for provisions. They left their mounts with a rancher and slipped into town, hoping to get passage on the stage.

The stage agent told them the stage would leave in the morning and that no passages were then being sold. However if they would leave their names, they would be entered in the waybill and could pay their fares in the morning.

"Enroll us as Jones and Smith," Howard said. "John and Joseph

Smith and Thomas and James Jones."

Hill Beachy was in the stage office at the time. He had heard of so many Smiths and Joneses in Lewiston that he took particular notice of the four men, their collars turned up, their hats pulled down on their heads, and mufflers covering all of their faces except the eyes.

When the four men checked into his Luna House, Beachy recognized three of them as ruffians who he heard had been with his friend at the Montana mines. Remembering his dream, he was suspicious that Magruder had met foul play. But Magruder's wife had recently got the message that her husband was leaving with a well guarded train. With no real evidence, Beachy, though angry and frustrated, could not detain the four before they took the morning stage to Walla Walla.

The discovery of Magruder's horse a few days later at the ranch where Howard had left it convinced Beachy that his friend was dead. The saddle was also identified as Magruder's.

The Territorial Governor happened to be in Lewiston, so Beachy got him to write requisitions on the governors of Oregon, Washington, and California. He started in pursuit at once, hiring a Tom Pike to help.

"I'm not a praying man," Beachy said later, "but the night before I left I just kneeled down and asked the Old Father to help me catch those fellows. I prayed for half an hour, and I prayed hard. I told Him that if He would help me just this once, I'd never ask Him for another favor as long as I lived — *and I never have!*"

When Beachy reached Walla Walla, he learned that the four men had taken a stage for Portland, saying they would catch the first steamer for San Francisco. They had displayed a lot of gold dust the few days they were there.

Sailing schedules down the Columbia River were infrequent, so Beachy and Pike took a stage to Portland. There, Pike was left to catch the next steamer, and Beachy took the stage from Portland to Sacramento.

After three days and nights of cooped-up travel, Beachy reached Yreka, the first place where he could telegraph San Francisco. He wired a description of the suspects to the San Francisco Chief of Police and requested their arrest under the authority of the governor's requisition.

The four men were in custody when Beachy reached San Francisco. Beachy waited for Pike and then waited still longer as Governor Leland Stanford studied the requisition from Idaho Territory, the first he had seen from there. After a four-week delay in the court, Beachy and Pike were allowed to leave with their prisoners.

When Beachy returned from his long trip for a friend, the enraged Idaho citizens wanted to hang the four men immediately.

"I told them they'd have a fair trial by jury," Beachy insisted. "I also promised that to the California authorities. I'll see they get their fair trial."

Idaho territory still had no laws on criminal procedure. On January 4, 1864, the legislature declared the common law of England in effect. The trial began the next day. Page had finally confessed, and was turned loose after he testified. He was soon killed, but no one knows by whom. Lowry, Howard, and Romaine were convicted of murder and sentenced to hang. The three prisoners were executed on March 4.

A detachment of soldiers from Fort Lapwai formed a hollow square around the convicted men to keep the crowd, estimated at ten thousand, from interfering with the hanging. A large group of Nez Perce Indians also came. Not understanding this strange white man's ritual, they watched closely, most in disbelief.

The territorial legislature, still in session, appropriated $6244 to reimburse Beachy for his expenses. The money found on the prisoners, together with what they had deposited in the San Francisco mint, was paid to Magruder's family.

The next spring Beachy led a party to the place where his friend had been killed. They found the victims in the gorge, where wolves had done their work. The men buried what remained. One skull, obviously Magruder's, had been split in two. Beachy also found the rusting Kentucky rifle he had given his friend. It had an unfired cartridge in the chamber.

Everything they found was consistent with Page's testimony, and everyone was finally certain that justice had been done. His dream had made Beachy certain from the beginning.

Although the killers were hanged by government authorities, they were punished for killings that were not crimes when done. This example and much of the history in what became Montana show that vigilantism in the Old West was as morally complex as many other areas of human behavior.

Hill Beachy, in his pursuit and capture, was a vigilante. He tried to follow law in obtaining the governor's requisition and in honoring his promise for a fair trial, but the necessary law never existed. Idaho Territory had no law when Magruder's party were killed.

Suggested reading: William J. McConnell, *Frontier Law: A Story of Vigilante Days* (New York: AMS Press, 1974).

IMPROPER VERDICT

Some time before 1883 a vigilante committee took two men accused of murder — but not yet tried in court — out of a Phoenix jail and hanged them in front of the town hall. Using two lumber wagons as scaffolds, the vigilantes drove the wagons out from under the prisoners after the nooses were in place. The first man either fainted or his noose was too tight; he strangled to death. Just as the team started forward with the second man, he leaped as high as he could, and his neck was broken in the fall.

"Why that son of a gun must have been hung before," one vigilante said. "He knows just how to do it."

After December, 1883, such vigilante action was largely replaced by legal executions. In that month Frank Heath led a gang of six men into the Sulphur Springs Valley, looking for places to rob.

Heath scouted ahead and then met the others outside Bisbee, where he briefed them on how to rob the Castañeda & Goldwater store.

While they robbed the store the gang killed an assayer, J. C. Tappinier, Deputy Sheriff D. T. Smith, and a Mrs. Roberts, and wounded two others. Then they rode out of town with their loot of twenty-five hundred dollars.

Heath was not present with the gang during the robbery and killings, but he met them outside town and got his share of the money. Then he joined the posse the next morning as it pursued the gang.

But Deputy Sheriff William Daniels learned of Heath's involvement and arrested him, along with the rest of the gang.

Heath came to trial first, and the jury found him guilty of second degree murder. The next morning a thirty-man mob from Bisbee and Tombstone took Heath out of the jail, hanged him from a telegraph pole, and threatened to hang the jury if they brought in any more verdicts like that.

Apparently the jury got the message. They found the other five gang members guilty of first degree murder and sentenced them all to be hanged. Their executions were the first legal hangings in Tombstone.

Suggested reading: William M. Breakenridge, *Helldorado* (Boston: Houghton Mifflin Co, 198).

PERHAPS A LITTLE TOO MUCH SHOOTING

I n 1864 a wealthy man named French who ranched on Leona Creek in South Texas murdered two Mexican cattle buyers. The men had crossed the Rio Grande with solid silver dollars, and French murdered them to get their money without having to sell any cattle.

One of French's vaquéros witnessed his employer's crime, and he related the details to Simons, a neighbor who didn't like French. Simons called in other neighbors. Over the objection of some who wanted an immediate hanging, they decided to take French to San Antonio and turn him over to the authorities.

They got French to San Antonio, but lost him to local vigilantes before they could surrender him to the law. The vigilantes, commanded by Hiram Minshul and Sol Chiff, had reportedly already hanged thirty men. They took French to the town plaza and hanged him from a chinaberry tree.

French's two sons, Jim and Dick, got home from Civil War service in the Texas Rangers just three days after their father had been carried off by the neighbors. They rode hard to San Antonio but arrived one day too late.

The brothers vowed to kill every man who had anything to do with their father's killing. Realizing the vigilantes were on the alert, the brothers decided to lay low a while as though the matter meant little to them.

French had been hanged in early November. To the surprise of the Nueces River ranchers, six months went by and the brothers had made no move. Many were astounded that the French boys had shown so little grit. The neighbors who had originally captured French were at their ease, because the brothers appeared as friendly as they had been before.

In late May 1865 news of the Confederacy's surrender reached Texas. Federal troops had taken charge in San Antonio, but in outlying areas every man was a law to himself. The French boys decided to start their crusade. But Minshul, Chiff, and the other vigilantes had by then fled to Mexico, so the first victims of the brothers' revenge were Simons and a friend of his, a man named Bishop.

The two men were out hunting cattle not far from where French had killed the cattle buyer. The French boys stole into their camp, roused them from their sleep, and gunned them down. Three of Simons' vaquéros fled, and the French brothers, knowing an alarm would result, hurried up Leona Creek to the McConnel ranch.

McConnel's two sons had served in the same ranger company with Jim and Dick French, but blood lust overpowered any sense of comradeship. The McConnel boys were out hunting cattle, but the French brothers killed the father, ate breakfast over his dead body, and set out for the Hays ranch, almost a day's ride away.

In late afternoon they met Hays riding toward them. Hays spun around and galloped homeward for dear life. After a hard ride, the brothers caught up to Hays and gunned down their fourth victim.

The next man on their list was named Stokes. The brothers learned that he had started for Eagle Pass with a bunch of cattle three weeks before. They rode easy, confident they would meet Stokes on his homeward journey, and that word of the killing spree would not have reached him.

About two weeks later, the French brothers met Stokes and his son nooning under some liveoak trees. They had heard nothing of the French boys' vendetta. Both men were shot down in cold blood, but only young Stokes had been killed. So the brothers hanged the wounded father on the tree under which lay his dead son.

The brothers then rode to Atascosa for Jake Peat, who, next to Simons, had been most prominent in the arrest of their father. Told that Peat was in Atascosa's only saloon, the boys rushed in, sixguns drawn, shouting, "Hands up!"

Now Jake Peat, a fighting kind of man, was talking to a friend made from the same substance. So when the other dozen men in the bar raised their hands, Peat and his friend whipped out their sixguns. But the brave men were too late, and both fell dead to the floor.

Apparently the brothers had now killed all the men who had originally arrested their father. We're not told exactly how many there were, but the victim list seemed to have three extra on it — Simons' friend, Stokes' son, and Peat's friend — who had not been involved in any way. Of course, the tragedy is that the arresting neighbors had taken French to San Antonio to be turned over to the legal authorities. The vigilantes who had hanged the man were still untouched.

After killing Jake Peat and his friend, the brothers ran into their old ranger company captain.

"I think you've done enough of this shooting business, and perhaps a little too much," Captain Williams said. "I advise you to get into Mexico as soon as you can."

"Just what we was figuring to do," Dick French replied. "We reckon we've about wiped out all of them as we wanted this side of the Rio Grande, and over there we're goin' to hunt around a bit for Hiram Minshul, Sol Chiff, and any of the gang we can find."

Williams never heard any more about his two former rangers. We don't know what they found in Mexico.

Suggested reading: R. H. Williams, *With the Border Ruffians* (Toronto: Musson Book Company, 1919).

IN A HURRY TO DANCE

Although Texas joined the Confederacy, the people of the state were about evenly divided on the question of secession. Eight men from Williamson County, reflecting that ambivalence, decided in July, 1863, that they didn't want to fight for either side. It was early in the month, and probably the news of Gettysburg, the bloodiest battle of the war, hadn't yet reached them. Nevertheless, they set out for Mexico, along with a young boy — perhaps the son of one of them — whose name we do not know.

All the men had good reputations and none were wanted by the law. When they reached Bandera, they stopped for a few days to lay in supplies. A frontier outpost, Bandera was twelve miles from Camp Verde, a military post which had fallen to Confederate troops shortly after the Civil War started.

When Major Alexander, commanding the post and its garrison of twenty-five cavalrymen, heard about the travelers, he sent a detail to capture them, saying they would stand military trial for desertion. Why the major thought civilians were subject to such prosecution is just one question in this affair, one of the most tragic in Texas' history.

The Williamson County men surrendered their arms on the promise that they would have a fair and impartial trial. Night overtook the cavalrymen and their eight prisoners on their way back to Camp Verde. They made camp about three miles from Bandera in a grove of oaks on the Julian River. The nearest cabin was a mile way.

After an early supper, the cavalrymen talked about riding back into Bandera to attend a dance.

"What will we do with these prisoners?" someone asked.

No one wanted to stand guard duty while his friends were in town whooping it up at the dance. After a heated discussion, someone said, "Why don't we just hang them and be done with it?"

The officer in charge didn't object, and some of the men began their plans, pointing out that a huge oak tree near their camp would be just right for the wholesale hanging.

But then other cavalrymen objected, saying it was inhuman and a violation of the promise that the prisoners would have a fair trial. After a heated argument, the cavalrymen opposed to the hanging saddled their horses and returned to Camp Verde.

With the objecting soldiers out of the way, the remaining soldiers, anxious to get to the dance, set to work. They found a long rope and dragged the frantic, protesting prisoners to the large oak.

The tree's majestic branches spread a serene canopy over the camp as the day's heat changed to an evening coolness. The sweet, haunting call of mockingbirds and the occasional yip of a coyote punctuated the soft night air. The natural setting of great beauty contrasted with the inhuman activity proceeding below.

The hangings were a botched mess. The man with the rope did not know how to use it, and no platform for a neck-breaking drop was used. The prisoners were taken, one by one, the rope fastened around the neck and the terrified man hauled from the ground in a prolonged, painful, strangling death. As each man was lowered, his body was shoved aside to make room for the next, and the macabre ritual continued.

One prisoner pleaded to be shot, and a soldier accommodated him. The young boy apparently disappeared with the murderers. No one knows who he was or what became of him.

The next day settler Joseph Poor, who lived on the Middle Verde River, was out looking for his horses when he came upon the shocking scene. Eight bodies lay where they had been shoved aside by men, hurrying to a dance. One of them had a ramrod protruding from the chest. The soldier who performed the mercy killing had forgotten to remove it after he loaded his musket. Poor thought it was an Indian arrow and he ran to Bandera with the alarm of Indians on the warpath.

A small party from Bandera rode out, recognized that it had not been an Indian attack, and scraped a community grave for the eight men from Williamson County. Later a backwoods tombstone was inscribed with the names C. J. Sawyer, W. M. Sawyer, William Shumake, George Thayer, Jack Whitmire, Jack Kyle, John Smart, and Van Winkle.

After the Civil War ended and the courts were again functioning, the Bandera County Grand Jury indicted Major Alexander and the soldiers responsible for the hangings. Warrants were issued and lawmen tried to serve them, but none of the defendants were ever found.

No one was brought to justice in one of Texas' greatest tragedies.

Suggested reading: Xanthus Carson, "Bandera's Eight Were Hung," in *Wild West*, January, 1972.

SETTLING ACCOUNTS

The sound of horses sliding to a stop outside Frank Eaton's cabin broke the stillness of that 1868 summer night on the Kansas prairie.

"Eaton — Frank Eaton," a coarse voice yelled. "Come on out."

"Don't go, Frank", Eaton's wife pleaded.

"Got to. Probably Mose Beaman and the boys coming for help."

Beaman headed the vigilantes, a group of northern men who protected citizens from the Regulators, a lawless band of southerners, some of whom had ridden with Quantrill during the Civil War. The Regulators rode at night, often disguised, to raid citizens and emigrant trains passing through. Frank Eaton, a Connecticut volunteer in the Union Army, had come to Kansas earlier that year, and was soon involved in the fighting.

But the riders outside the Eaton cabin were Regulators, not vigilantes. They gunned Eaton down in cold blood.

Eight-year-old Frank, Junior, heard the gunfire and his mother's scream and saw his father collapse outside the door. He ran outside and threw himself on his father's bloody, bullet-riddled body.

"Remember that, you damn Yankees," someone shouted as the killers rode into the night.

Little Frank Eaton remembered. He had seen the faces in the moonlight — four Clampseys and two Ferbers. The sobbing boy burned the faces into his memory and then muttered a solemn oath, "I'll get even, Pa. I'll get even."

Mose Beaman gave little Frank his first pistol, a heavy Navy revolver with an eight-inch barrel. For two years the boy practiced drawing and firing, first with one hand, then with the other. By then his mother had remarried, and the family lived in Indian Territory near Fort Gibson.

The 6th Cavalry, stationed at the fort, liked the boy. The soldiers let him join in their shooting competitions. The cavalrymen shot well, but Frank was better. The colonel called him Pistol Pete.

In 1875, when Frank was fifteen, he became a cowboy. He heard about rustlers disposing of their stolen stock through Shannon Clampsey and Doc Ferber, who lived by the Canadian River. This was the first he had heard about any of his father's murderers.

Shannon Clampsey sat on the porch of his cabin, a rifle across his lap, when Frank rode up.

"Stop where you are, kid," Clampsey shouted. "Who are you and what do you want?"

"I didn't think you'd recognize me, Shan. I was just a little tyke when you killed my pa."

Clampsey had his rifle up in a split second, but it was a split second too late. He died before he could fire the weapon.

Frank looked about quickly for Doc Ferber. He saw a trail leading up a ravine and followed. Suddenly Ferber rode out of some trees.

"Hello, boy," Ferber said as he reached for his gun. "I thought I heard a shot."

Ferber fell from his horse, two bullet holes in his chest.

Frank learned that the rustlers had been selling the stolen cattle in Missouri through John Ferber. The night before Frank arrived in John Ferber's town, Ferber was shot and killed for dealing off the bottom of a poker deck.

Frank learned that Jim and Jonce Clampsey had a little ranch in the Ozarks, a day's ride away. He reached their cabin just before supper time. Jonce was outside washing his hands.

"Is this where Jim and Jonce Clampsey live?" Frank asked.

Jonce nodded.

"Are you Jim?" Frank needed to know where the second man was before the shooting started.

"I'm Jonce."

"I've got a message for Jim from John Ferber, who was shot a couple nights ago."

Jim Clampsey came out the cabin door, his rifle in his hand. "I'm Jim. What did John say to tell me?"

"I'm Frank Eaton. I'm going to kill both of you."

Jonce reached for his pistol and Jim swung the rifle up. Jim died like his brother, Shannon, the unfired rifle under his body. Jonce got one shot off, but it plowed into the ground as he fell.

Frank continued cowboying, working part of the time for Charles Goodnight. He became a deputy marshal. Ten years after killing Jim and Jonce Clampsey, he learned that Wyley Clampsey was tending bar in Albuquerque.

Wyley had a bodyguard on each side when Frank walked into the bar.

"Go for your gun, Wyley."

Wyley died with two bullets in his chest. Each bodyguard got one bullet into Frank before someone shot out the lights. The wounds were not serious. Frank Eaton soon recovered, satisfied that now the accounts were finally settled.

Frank Eaton, *Pistol Pete, veteran of the Old West* (New York: Little Brown, 1952).

GIVE THE MAN AIR!

J ohanna Londrigan, the woman in the triangle, left her Rhode Island home in the 1860s to live with a married sister in Chicago. After stops in San Francisco and Virginia City, Nevada, she opened a laundry in Bodie, California, in 1878, doing some catering on the side.

In Bodie Johanna met and married Thomas Treloar, a Cornish miner who had been in the West a dozen years. Treloar, a small, harmless man, had been little more than half-witted following a 225-foot fall down a mine shaft in Virginia City.

Johanna also found Joseph DeRoche in Bodie. A French-Canadian acquaintance from her Chicago days, DeRoche owned a brickyard on the edge of town. The townspeople gossiped about a romance, and Treloar burned with jealousy. The triangle was complete.

On Thursday, January 13, 1881, Johanna was catering a ball for a social society at the Miner's Union Hall. Sometime after midnight Treloar came by the ball and saw his wife dancing with DeRoche.

"I told her to not dance with that man," he complained to the doorman. "She said she wouldn't."

The doorman warned Treloar, obviously agitated, to not cause trouble.

"She's been untrue," Treloar said. "I'll kill that man."

The threat was passed on to DeRoche.

"If he starts anything, I'll kill him," DeRoche said.

Treloar returned when the ball ended, but he left with DeRoche, not with his wife. As they walked down the street, witnesses saw DeRoche pull a .38 caliber revolver from his pocket, fall a step behind, and shoot Treloar in the back of the head.

When Johanna left the ball she walked down the street and saw DeRoche in the custody of Deputy Sheriff James Monahan. Her husband, lying in a pool of blood, died at her feet.

Monahan delivered DeRoche to the constable at the jail about two o'clock. Two hours later another deputy rushed in to say that a lynch mob was gathering outside.

The officers rushed to DeRoche's cell and unlocked it.

"What are you trying to do?" the prisoner asked. "Hang me?"

"No, we're trying to save you." They conferred about a safe place to take the prisoner.

But one of the deputies was drunk, and in the confusion DeRoche escaped. Bodie citizens were incensed with both the murder and the escape. They knew that Treloar was a quiet, peaceable man who never carried a gun. A coroner's jury returned a verdict of willful and premeditated murder, and the search was on.

At the funeral service on Saturday, the minister appealed to God to strike down the assassin. "If a man has an irresistible impulse to take another's life," he preached, "I say let the law have an irresistible impulse to put a rope around his neck."

The search intensified. Many of the citizens were military veterans, and they organized into squads with officers and a regular chain of command. They rounded up DeRoche's friends and grilled them. Not until they put a noose over the head of one friend and threatened to hang him did they learn where the fugitive was.

But, surprisingly, the vigilantes returned DeRoche to the jail. Then followed a long discussion about waiting for the law to take its course or proceeding with an early hanging. Just after lawyer Pat Reddy finished an impressive speech advocating caution, the Sunday paper came out with an editorial which fanned the flames of outrage again.

That afternoon, the justice court held its examination. Advised of his right to counsel, DeRoche said he'd take Pat Reddy, Bodie's leading defense lawyer.

"I'm already hired to prosecute the case," Reddy said.

By the end of the hearing, Bodie citizens decided that DeRoche had had enough justice. Shortly after midnight several hundred armed vigilantes took him out of the jail and marched him in company formation to a hoisting frame in front of the backsmith shop. Snow had begun to fall, and the moon shed a pale glow on the improvised gallows.

"Let's move it to where he killed Treloar," shouted a vigilante. Several men picked up the hoisting frame and carried it to the place of the murder.

They slipped the noose over his head and jerked DeRoche off the ground. As DeRoche choked for air and his legs twitched in his death throes, an onlooker with a grotesque sense of humor was heard to say:

"Keep back! Give the man all the air he needs."

Suggested reading: Roger D. McGrath, *Gunfighters, Highwaymen, and Vigilantes* (Berkeley: University of California Press, 1984).

UNLUCKY HITCH HIKER

James "Kid" Hall, nineteen, had become so disreputable in Deadwood and Crook City that the South Dakota citizens ordered him out of town in June, 1877. He was walking south on a hot, dusty trail when A. J. "Doc" Allen and Louis "Red" Curry, both in their thirties, overtook him as they drove six stolen horses along the trail. Hall looked so pitiable they invited him to mount up and ride with them. He gladly accepted their kind invitation and rode along with his new companions, whom he had never seen before.

A few days later, Dave Markel from Rapid City was cutting building logs out in the woods when he saw the three men and the stolen horses. He hurried back to town as though he were Paul Revere with an impending massacre to prevent. He told Sheriff Frank Moulton what he had seen.

The sheriff raised a large posse, and they galloped out of town, determined to kill someone. Capturing the three men, who were napping in the shade with the horses tied nearby, was easy.

"You bastards wouldn't have got us if we hadn't been asleep," Hall growled. The thieves kept quiet, hoping for the best.

The posse locked the prisoners in a stage barn at the east end of town. Hall showered the sheriff and his deputies with curses, adding comments about the morals of their ancestors. As the posse joined in the verbal brawl, they seemed to have forgotten Allen and Curry, both of whom were very quiet.

Justice of the peace Bob Burleigh held the preliminary hearing that evening. Both Allen and Curry admitted guilt and said that Hall had nothing to do with the horse stealing.

"We just rode up on him on our way to Rapid City," they said. "We tuk pity on him, limping along in the dust and we offered him a ride. He didn't know nothing about the horses being stolen."

But Burleigh knew about Hall's bad reputation, and he bound all three over to the circuit court for trial. No written record was made of the preliminary hearing.

That same night at midnight a band of masked men surrounded the barn where the prisoners were being held. "Of course the guards were compelled to surrender them, and to accompany the visiting committee," the report, written later about the incident, said.

The three men were marched up a hill to a lone pine tree, and Allen and Curry made to stand on low rock piles as nooses were dropped into place. The masked men kicked the rocks away, and the two horse thieves strangled to death.

"What do we do with the kid?" someone asked.

"Dead men tell no tales," replied another. "I say string him up with the others."

In a few minutes Kid Hall, loudly protesting his innocence, was also struggling and kicking the air as the life squeezed out of his young body.

The next morning Justice Burleigh held his coroner's inquest in the midst of the three bodies, still hanging from the tree, their faces black, their tongues protruding. Then bystanders cut the bodies down and buried them.

Sometime later Henry Curry, father of "Red," came looking for his son's body and an explanation of what had happened. Justice Burleigh assured him that his son and Allen had admitted stealing the horses. He mentioned that everyone had heard the confessions while the men were exonerating Kid Hall. Warned that if he wanted to get home safely he should leave town at once, Henry Curry took the advice.

The report of the incident ended: "The hanging of the three unprincipled characters had a very wholesome effect on the unruly element and placed a very effective damper on cattle rustling and horse stealing."

The hill where the hangings occurred has been called Hangman's Hill ever since. Some residents of Rapid City were still remembering Kid Hall's loud, curse-filled protestations of innocence over thirty years later. He was certainly South Dakota's unluckiest hitch hiker.

Suggested reading: Jesse Brown and A. M. Willard, *The Black Hills Trails*, (Rapid City: Rapid City Journal Co., 1924).

VIGILANTE HORSE RACE

Fort Griffin, Texas, in 1878 was one of the roughest places on the frontier. Besides the soldiers at the nearby fort, buffalo hunters, cowboys, sporting women, gamblers, and desperadoes of all kinds crowded into the Flat, a lawless area around the town, for their wild celebrations. City Marshall John W. Poe tried to control the rough element with his deputies, but a third faction, the vigilantes, were convinced the machinery of law did not work in that lawless country along the Clear Fork of the Brazos River. Poe thought the regular processes of law, even if imperfect, were better than the summary measures of vigilantes. The John Laren incident showed the tension between the three factions.

Laren had come to Fort Griffin in about 1870. He said he was from Mobile, Alabama, and had run away from home, ending up on a ranch near Trinidad, Colorado. He said his boss refused to pay him, so he took a horse for his pay and struck out for Texas. When the boss caught up with him, Laren beat him to the draw and claimed that he had killed the man in self defense.

But a saloon keeper, who came from Colorado shortly after Laren, said Laren had stolen the horse and shot his boss down in cold blood.

Laren got a job on Joe Matthews' ranch, and, in about a year, married the boss' daughter, Mary. At first the family objected, saying they knew nothing about Laren. But after the wedding Joe Matthews helped his son-in-law build a ranch house, and Laren started running a brand of his own.

In 1876 Laren and his closest friend, John Selman, decided that the Throckmorton County sheriff could be defeated. With the help of residents of the Flat, they got Laren elected sheriff. Then he appointed Selman his chief deputy.

After a short time, people began to wonder about their sheriff. For one thing, Laren got a contract to supply three beeves a day to the military garrison at the fort. Ranchers noticed that their herds were being reduced by exactly that amount, and Laren's herd stayed the same size. Even Joe Matthews and Laren's brother-in-law complained about losing cattle. Although nothing was ever proved, the suspicion was enough to get Bill Cruger elected sheriff at the next election.

Poe, by then a deputy U. S. marshal as well as city marshal of Fort Griffin, was also appointed a Throckmorton County deputy sheriff. The citizens, including Laren's father-in-law, asked Sheriff Cruger to investigate the ranchers' loss of cattle.

About this time, a homesteader named Lancaster suggested that the sheriff drag a deep hole in the Clear Fork, near Laren's corrals. Using grappling hooks, Poe and other deputies recovered two hundred cowhides. None had Laren's brand; all had brands from other area ranchers.

Shortly after talking to the sheriff, Lancaster disappeared. His wife asked the sheriff to look for him. They found him seriously wounded, hiding in the brakes along the river. Reluctant at first to talk, he finally said he had been chased away and wounded by Laren and Selman.

Sheriff Cruger moved cautiously after getting his warrants. He knew that Laren and Selman had many friends among the lawless element of the county. He assembled a large posse which slipped up on Laren's ranch during the night. They waited quietly for dawn.

Laren made his capture easy. He came out of the house with a milk pail but no gun. Cruger made the arrest, and the posse took Laren to Albany, the county seat, fourteen miles south of Fort Griffin.

But Cruger worried about the reaction of the residents of the Flat as they rode through it on their way to Albany. He suspected Selman was already gathering a crowd of gunmen to spring Laren loose.

Albany had no jail, and the sheriff had to put his prisoner in a private house under close guard. He stopped at a blacksmith shop and had shackles riveted to Laren's legs. Sure that Laren's friends were up to something, Cruger took no chances.

Then the third element entered the picture — the Fort Griffin Vigilance Committee. They also expected Selman and other friends of Laren to attempt a rescue. They decided that if Laren was freed, the county would be embroiled in a civil war. They set out for Albany in a fourteen-mile race with Selman's gang of thugs. The vigilantes won.

Poe captained the guard for the first watch. Shortly before midnight — it was Sunday, June 23 — he stepped out of the house, and the vigilantes overpowered him and his guards.

As the vigilantes moved into the makeshift jail, all the inmates knew why they had come. They moved as far from Laren as their chains allowed. "What do you want?" Laren demanded, facing the masked men. "You," the vigilante chief said. "It's time to cash in your checks. You played up to the decent people of this county, and all the time you've been running with the scum that's been doing all the dirty work. What do you have to say?"

"Not a damn thing to your cowardly gang. You sneaked up here and captured the sheriff's guards after he promised me a fair trial. Take my irons off and give me a gun and I'll fight your whole outfit. That gang of yours will need a new boss in about two seconds."

The vigilante chief talked to some of his men as Laren waited, defiance written across his face.

"All right," the chief said. "You did do some good things while you were sheriff, so we're not going to hang you. We'll just use our guns, instead."

The chief turned to the masked men behind him. Then he jerked his head toward Laren and said, "All right, boys, step up and do your duty."

Eleven men moved forward and quietly raised their Winchesters.

"Come on," Laren yelled at the masked intruders. "Shoot me to hell as quickly as you can."

The volley of rifle fire roared out the firing squad's answer. Mary Laren, keeping a lonely vigil in the Shields Hotel across the street, ran from her room, screaming.

"Oh, they've killed him," she shouted. "My poor dear John. I'll never see him again."

Selman's gang had just reached the edge of Albany when they heard the shots ringing out the chorus of Laren's death.

"It's no use, boys," Selman yelled to his men. "The damned stranglers beat us to it. It's our necks we got to think about now. Let's get out of town."

The gang whirled around and rode away in the darkness. The vigilantes chased them but were unable to get within rifle shot.

The vigilantes did perform one more chore on that dark night. At daybreak the body of a man was found swinging from a tree on the Clear Fork. No one knew who he was or why he had been hanged.

Suggested reading: Sophia A. Poe, *Buckboard Days* (Albuquerque: Univ. of New Mexico Press, 1964).

43

DESPERATE CHARACTERS

Virginia-born Granville Stuart was four when his parents took up a claim in Iowa. He grew up there, and went to California in 1852 with his father and brother James. In 1857, now twenty-two, he and James migrated to Idaho Territory (present Montana) to try their luck. They were in on the first discovery of gold, and Granville followed a prospector's and trader's life until 1879, when he started ranching. He established his home ranch in the Judith Mountains, near where the army later built Fort Maginnis. .

After spring roundup in 1881, Granville estimated his livestock losses at five percent from raiding Indians, five percent from predatory animals, and three percent from storms. But after the fall roundup in 1883, Granville's losses from rustlers were at least three percent. A nearby rancher's cows invariably had twin calves, sometimes triplets. Honest ranchers told the man they woud hang him if his cows kept having twins.

At the second annual meeting of the Montana Stock Growers' Association in April, 1884, many members wanted to take direct action against the rustlers. They included Theodore Roosevelt, North Dakota rancher who belonged to the association, and his neighbor the Marquis DeMores. Both men were close friends of Granville Stuart, but he advocated caution, saying the fight would take many lives. Stuart's conservative views carried the day, and the association voted to take no formal action.

But at that year's spring roundup, rustlers stole a valuable stallion, many other good horses, and twenty-four head of beef steers from Stuart's range. When they realized they could not escape Stuart's cowhands, the rustlers drove the cattle into a coulee, killed them all, and left the meat to spoil.

Knowing that rustlers were camped on his range at the mouth of the Musselshell, at Rocky Point, and at Wolf Point, the outraged Stuart was now ready to join other ranchers in a war of self defense. He appeared to be a leader of Montana's second organization of vigilantes.

On June 25, Narciss Lavardure and Joe Vardner watched a herder leave his camp to look for strays. Then they cut out seven saddle horses and drove them off. But a neighbor recognized the horses and ordered the rustlers to stop. In the six-mile race and shootout that followed, the neighbor, William Thompson, killed Vardner and captured Lavardure. That night an armed posse overpowered Thompson and hanged Larvardure.

On July 3, Sam McKenzie was caught in a canyon a few miles above Fort Maginnis with two stolen horses. That night he was hanged from a cottonwood tree.

Also on July 3, Stuart, while out range riding, met up with two tough looking characters, camped at a spring. Edward Owen had long unkempt hair, small, shifty eyes, and a cruel mouth. He and his partner, Charles (Rattlesnake Jake) Fallon, each wore two forty-four revolvers and a hunting knife. Stuart decided to keep an eye on them while they were on his range. The next day Ben Cline rode by the camp of the two men, leading a horse he intended to enter in the races at Lewistown. Rattlesnake Jake challenged Cline to a race. Cline was reluctant because he wanted to keep the horse fresh for Lewistown, but they bantered him into the race which Cline's horse won. Then the two men saddled up and rode to Lewistown themselves for the Fourth of July festivities.

Rattlesnake Jake and Owen got to Lewistown in time for the races, but their delay in Crowley's saloon kept them from the track until the last race. They bet that one heavily, lost, and were in an ugly mood back at the saloon.

Bob Jackson, a young man in an Uncle Sam costume who had been in the parade that morning, somehow was offensive to Owen, who clubbed him to the ground with his revolver. Then he placed his cocked revolver to Jackson's head and made him crawl like a snake.

"Well, I guess we'll clean out this town," Owen sneered to Rattlesnake Jake. He shot randomly into the crowd, but did not hit anyone. They returned to the saloon for more drinks, then swaggered out into the street, declaring they were ready to clean out the town.

But several citizens, sensing trouble, had armed themselves with Winchesters and were waiting from hidden positions along the street. Joe Doney shot Owen in the stomach with a twenty-two caliber revolver as Owen crossed the street. Doney ran into the saloon, and other men in the street opened up on Rattlesnake Jake. Jake looked back, saw that Owen was wounded, and ran toward him through a shower of lead. On the way, he dropped to one knee and shot at Joseph Jackson and Ben Smith, two young men who were crossing the street. He wounded Jackson twice and killed Smith.

When the smoke cleared, Rattlesnake Jake had nine wounds and Owen eleven, any one of which would have been fatal.

That afternoon Stuart got a telegram from Buffalo, Wyoming, stating that Rattlesnake Jake and Owen were desperate characters and wanted at several places. They had stolen horses in Wyoming. Later he learned that Owen was wanted for murder in Louisiana, and Rattesnake Jake was wanted in New Mexico for shooting up a ranch and burning haystacks.

That evening a vigilante committee visited Billy Downs' place at the mouth of the Musselshell, which had become headquarters for the tough characters in that area. Downs met the committee in company with

GRANVILLE STUART

Montana Historical Society

California Ed, another notorious character. They admitted stealing horses from Indians but denied stealing from whites. However they failed to explain how twenty-six horses got into their corrals, all bearing well-known brands of white ranchers.

Downs' house was full of salted meat, ready for shipment downriver. He said it was buffalo, although the northern bufalo herd had been gone for two years. The vigilantes found a stack of fresh cowhides, all bearing the brand of the Fergus Stock Company. They took Downs and California Ed to a nearby grove of trees and hanged them.

On July 8, nine vigilantes arrived at Bates point, fifteen miles on downstream. Here lived Old Man Jones, his two sons and a nephew. Six other thieves lived in a tent nearby. The vigilantes waited for daybreak and the shooting started.

The vigilantes set fire to the cabin. The men inside kept firing from portholes until they were either killed by gunfire or burned to death.

The tent was surrounded by thick brush, making escape easier. One man slipped out to a dense clump of willows, where he made his last stand. Another dropped into a dry well and wasn't found until dark. Four others, two of them wounded, escaped. But they were soon captured by soldiers, who turned them over to the U. S. marshal.

A party of vigilantes intercepted the marshal, taking his prisoners from him at a place where two cabins stood close together. The four men were promptly hanged from a log that reached between the cabins. The cabin was then burned down and the bodies cremated.

One hundred sixty-five stolen horses were recovered at Bates Point, and one hundred nineteen at other places. Then the vigilantes disbanded and returned to their homes. There was no more horse or cattle stealing in Montana for many years.

Granville Stuart was twice elected to the Montana Territorial Council, serving one term as president. President Cleveland appointed him Minister to Uruguay and Paraguay. Later he was commissioned by Montana to write its history. He did not live to complete the book, but he had lived an important part of that history, including the elimination of the outlaw problem in one violent summer in 1884.

Stuart and his first wife, an Indian woman, had nine children. After she died, he married a white woman, with whom he lived until his death in 1918, aged eighty-four.

Suggested reading: Granville Stuart, *Forty Years on the Frontier* (Cleveland: The Arthur Clarke Co., 1925).

A HANGING AT INDEPENDENCE ROCK

Ella Watson, twenty-five-year-old daughter of a Kansas farmer, was working in a bawdy house in Rawlins, Wyoming, in 1886. There she met Jim Averell, who was running a road ranch on the Sweetwater, where the Rawlins-Lander stage line crossed the Oregon Trail.

Earlier that year, Averell had filed a homestead claim on a quarter section right in the middle of the range claimed by Albert J. Bothwell. Bothwell was the most arrogant of the ranchers in the Sweetwater Valley, and he was determined to throw Averell off his ranch. But Averell was abrasive, and he enjoyed making Bothwell mad.

Averell, a well educated man, wrote letters to newspapers around the state, constantly criticizing local cattlemen for their high-handed methods in fighting homesteaders and sheepherders. He brought Ella to the Sweetwater to open a "hog ranch" next to his road ranch, thus enlarging the range of services available to his customers. In addition, she brightened Averell's personal life. Within a few weeks, Ella also filed on a homestead claim near Averell's. Bothwell was furious.

Ella was full-bosomed and not bad looking. She had gone west and "gone wrong," but the cowboys that patronized Averell's establishment had no complaints. Ella was a sharp-tongued strumpet, a good partner for Averell. When Averell condemned Bothwell and other ranchers as land grabbing tryants and despoilers of the public domain, Ella, also a loud critic of the stockmen, added her own colorful vocabulary. Bothwell tried several times to buy her out of her homestead claim; she told him in plain terms where he could stuff his money.

Averell never owned any cattle, but Ella soon acquired enough that she hired a cowboy, John De Carey, to work for her. She also built a house, barns, corrals, and fences, and improved her claim. Three years later, she had a nice little ranch, right in the middle of Bothwell's large spread. The rancher, unable to buy Ella out, turned desperate.

On Saturday, July 20, 1889, Ella and her cowboy took a wagon down to the river to buy some beadwork and moccasins from Indians camped there. They returned to find Bothwell and five cowboys cutting Ella's fence and driving her cattle away. When Ella protested, Bothwell told her to shut up and get in the wagon; they were taking her back to Rawlins. Outnumbered and outgunned, Ella did as she was told.

Bothwell and his men found Averell nearby and forced him into the wagon.

"Where is your warrant?" demanded Averell.

Bothwell and John Durbin drew their revolvers. "This is warrant enough for you damn squatters," growled Bothwell.

ELLA WATSON

Wyoming Division of Cultural Resources

Averell also got into the wagon.

Gene Crowder, a fourteen-year-old boy who witnessed the abduction, rode to Averell's road ranch and told the customers what had happened. Only one cowboy had courage enough to act.

Frank Buchanan, armed only with a revolver, jumped on his horse and followed Bothwell and his men. He saw them rounding Independence Rock, the famous landmark on the Oregon Trail. He caught up with them in a sagebrush gulch, containing a few, scraggly cottonwood trees. They had a noose around Averell's neck and were trying to get one on Ella. She kept twisting and dodging, and Bothwell's men cursed her as they struggled.

Buchanan opened fire and emptied his pistol twice. But the vigilantes' rifle fire forced the cowboy to retreat. He went back to the road ranch and reported the hangings. Then he rode on to Casper to get the sheriff.

By the time a posse had been formed and led back by Buchanan, the bodies had dangled side by side in the hot July sun for almost three days. It was obvious that Ella and Averell had strangled slowly.

Ella sometimes used the name, Kate Maxwell. She was the first "Cattle Kate". That name was used later for other women who seemed to enlarge their cattle herds by gifts from cowboys, grateful for favors bestowed.

Bothwell, Durbin, and the other cowboys were indicted for the murders. They were defended by the attorneys for the Wyoming Stockgrowers' Association. By the time the case came to trial, all the witnesses, including Frank Buchanan, John De Carey, and Gene Crowder, had disappeared. Some witnesses were found dead under mysterious circumstances. The six indicted men went free.

Albert Bothwell still reigned supreme as lord of the Sweetwater Valley.

Suggested reading: Helena H. Smith, *The War on Powder River* (New York: McGraw-Hill, 1966).

ESCAPE FROM VIGILANTES

The fear which some had of vigilantes is well shown by an 1881 incident in Las Vegas, New Mexico Territory. Joe Ebright, gambler and hired gunman, had come to Las Vegas from Denver. He worked as bartender at Bertha's Parlor and Saloon and, more importantly, became the "solid man" for Bertha Kline, the madam and proprietor. About nine o'clock on the morning of March 23, Ebright was on duty when Jim Curry entered the bar.

Curry, a freight conductor on the southern division of the Santa Fe Railroad, was a popular man in the growing railroad town, but he had been robbed in the street the night before and, between his hangover and his anger, he was on the prod for trouble. Just after Joe served Curry his whiskey, Jim Thora, standing near Curry at the bar, ordered another drink. He laid a frayed and torn bill on the bar for payment, and Ebright expressed some reluctance at taking it. Perhaps he thought Thora had enough.

"That money is good enough to spend in a place like this," Curry said.

"What the hell business is it of yours?" Ebright snapped.

The verbal argument between the bartender and his nosy customer proceeded through several levels of inflamed cursing and ended with Curry drawing on Ebright. "I'll kill you, you son of a bitch," Curry snarled.

Ebright ducked down and grabbed his British Bull Dog pistol from its secret compartment under the bar. Just then Bertha walked in from her room in the rear, saw Curry pointing his gun at her lover, and screamed.

Curry whirled, threw down on Bertha, and shouted, "Shut up, you slut, or I'll kill you, too."

With that, Ebright peeked over the bar and fired, hitting Curry in the head.

In the few minutes it took Curry to bleed to death, the bar filled with townseople, many of them railroad workers who held the victim in high esteem. He had come to the territory from the Texas Pacific Railroad, and had already received a couple of promotions. His daughter had just graduated from a female seminary in Illinois. Until very recently, Curry had had no drinking problem.

Judge William Steele shoved his way into the bar, announced that he'd tolerate no vigilante justice in his town, instructed Sheriff Segura to arrest Ebright, and immediately picked a coroner's jury.

The jury ruled that Ebright had fired in self defense, but by this time Curry's friends had gathered at the Baptist Chapel to view the body and talk about a hanging. Probably for his own protection, Ebright was kept in custody. In spite of the coroner's verdict, Ebright was charged with murder.

The outcome makes one suspect that filing the charges was for his protection, also.

Curry was buried on Thursday, March 24. Two days later Justice of the Peace Jose Montoya presided at Ebright's preliminary hearing on the murder charge. The case took little time as no one appeared to prosecute. After testimony from Ebright, Bertha, and two witnesses who had served on the coroner's jury, Montoya held the evidence insufficient to require Ebright to stand trial and he ordered him released. All witnesses had agreed that Curry was holding a cocked pistol in his hand when Ebright shot him.

Then Ebright was immediately charged with disturbing the peace, probably to keep him in custody a little longer. The growing crowd kept talking about taking him up to the windmill. A windmill in the plaza center had become a favorite gibbet for the vigilantes.

Later on March 26, Ebright was brought before Judge Steele for his trial on the misdemeanor charge of disturbing the peace. To no one's surprise the judge found him not guilty, but Bertha had used the additional time her lover was in custody to make plans for getting him safely out of town.

Bertha worked out an escape plan with a friend, Moise. Moise hid a horse about four miles out of town. He waited there while Bertha hired a public hack to take her to the jail at 6:30 that evening, probably when most of the vigilantes were wetting their throats for supper.

As the hack drew up in front of the jail, Ebright dashed out, jumped in, and they raced out of town. When they reached the hidden horse, Joe gave Bertha a quick kiss and hug.

Then the man who had been found blameless by the coroner's jury, the justice of the peace, and the trial judge counted his blessings, leaped into the saddle, and rode off into the sunset, safe from the feared vigilantes. With that, history closed its book on Joe Ebright.

Vigilante use of the plaza center windmill continued so frequently that the owner eventually dismantled it.

Suggested reading: Bob L'Aloge, *Knights of the Sixgun*, (Las Cruces: Yucca Tree Press, 1991).

TYPICAL VIGILANTE REIGN

Barney Prine, settling in 1877 at the intersection of Ochoco Creek and Crooked River in Oregon, was the first resident of what became Prinevile, the county seat of Crook County. Five years later the community had a deputy sheriff but still little experience with organized law. Prineville's short vigilante reign was probably typical of many Old West communities.

The vigilante experience started in March, 1882, when old settler Lucius Langdon killed two neighbors, A. H. Crooks and Steven Jury, with whom he had been quarreling over boundaries. Another neighbor, Garret Maupin, heard Langdon's two shots and he saw Langdon riding home with his rifle. Maupin found the bodies of the victims, but no one else was around.

The coroner's jury had its hearing and went to Langdon's house to question him. The suspect was not there, but a man named W. H. Harrison was. The jury returned to Prineville and a posse formed to search for Langdon.

Langdon was found at his brother's cabin, about seventeen miles away.

In the meantime, the justice of the peace issued a warrant for Harrison who had been staying with Langdon before the murders. Harrison gloated over the fact that the troublemakers had been killed, but there was apparently nothing else to tie him to the crime.

Both Langdon and Harrison were brought to town about two in the morning and turned over to Deputy Sheriff J. L. Lukey. Lukey, having no jail, kept the prisoners under guard in the hotel, and he kept Langdon shackled.

About five that morning Lukey was overpowered from behind, thrown to the floor and blindfolded. Immediately he heard four or five pistol shots, followed by a groan. He could tell by the cries that Harrison was being hurried from the room. After he heard the hotel doors close, Lukey got up, removed the blindfold, and saw that Langdon had been shot to death. After daylight he discovered that Harrison had been hanged from the Crooked River bridge.

Lukey seemed relieved that his responsibilities had ended less than twenty-four hours after the murders of Langdon's neighbors. He wrote a friend: "I feel conscious of having done my duty as an officer so there I let the matter rest."

But the Vigilante Committee didn't rest. The next Christmas eve they killed Al Swartz while he was playing poker. The only reason ever given was that he had "defied" the committee.

On the same Christmas eve, the vigilantes shot two young men named Ludstrom and Housten, who were staying with J. M. Barns. After being shot, the young men were dragged to a tree and hanged.

Ludstrom was killed because of a dispute between him and Barnes about wages. Housten, a jockey, had agreed to throw a race, but then bet sixty dollars on his own horse and rode it to win.

The next spring Barns had a saloon argument with Mike Mogan over a six dollar debt. He told Mogan he'd shoot him right then if he didn't pay. Mogan refused to pay, and Barns shot him to death. While this was not vigilante action, it was clearly the action of a vigilante, who proved that he thought he was above the law.

That December, less than a year after the three Christmas Eve executions, Mike Mogan's brother Frank got into a saloon argument over wages with Bud Thompson. Thompson slipped up behind Frank Mogan and killed him with a shot to the back of the head.

The grand jury refused to act, showing how completely the vigilantes had assumed control of the community. Thompson, later a prominent newspaperman in the state, went unpunished. Frank Mogan's widow got a judgment against him for killing her husband, but was never able to collect.

But the people had had enough, and a new committee was formed to resist the vigilantes and turn the administration of justice back to the court system. They called the new committee the Moonshiners. By the 1884 election, the Moonshiners carried almost the whole ticket, and the reign of the vigilantes had ended.

Most people thought that Frank Mogan was the last man killed by vigilantes in the Prineville community. But a few years later a human skeleton was found hanging from a tree twelve miles south of Prineville. Unidentified, it appeared to be another vigilante hanging from the time the group was in power.

Suggested reading: Elton Carey, "Reign of the Vigilantes," in *Frontier Times* (January, 1970).

INDIAN VENGEANCE

Poker Tom had been missing since mid-April, 1891. Now, on June 2, a delegation of his Paiute tribesmen from their Walker River Reservation in Nevada called on other Paiutes at Bridgeport, California, for help in finding him. Captain Charlie, leader of the Nevada Paiutes, told Captain Jim of the Bridgeport group that they knew Poker Tom had played cards in Bridgeport with Chinese merchant, Ah Quong Tai, winning fifty dollars. Later Poker Tom bought some calico and told the storekeeper he was going home before he lost the rest of his winnings.

"We heard he went back to play some more," Captain Jim said. "Nobody's seen him since."

A thorough search north of town, where Poker Tom usually staked his horse, produced his saddle blanket and the bundle of calico. The Indians turned this evidence over to Sheriff M. J. Cody and continued their search. They swore to wreak vengeance on Ah Tai if he had killed Poker Tom. Sheriff Cody, whom they respected, got their promise to make no disturbance that night.

Two days later the Indians dragged the river, finding Poker Tom's water-logged coat. The sheriff then searched Ah Tai's store. In the back room, used for gambling, he found floorboards showing recent scrubbings. He also found new wrapping paper on the walls which, when removed, revealed blood stains underneath.

Ah Tai admitted playing poker with Poker Tom the night he disappeared. He claimed to know nothing more.

Two days later the dragging of the river produced a human torso. With no head, no arms, and cut off just below the waist, the gender could not even be determined. But the distraught Paiutes were convinced it was their missing tribesman. Medical examination showed that the trunk had been pickled, or "salted down as though for corned beef."

Some Bridgeport Indians then remembered that in eating at Ah Tai's store they had been served a strange, pickled meat with a sweet taste.

"What is it?" they had asked.

"Goat," Ah Tai had said.

Further search by the sheriff found empty brine barrels in Ah Tai's cellar. The anger of the Indians, convinced now that Ah Tai had fed them part of their own tribesman, reached war-path pitch. They demanded that the sheriff turn the Chinaman over to them.

The sheriff talked about due process of law. The Indians reminded him that they had recently turned over an Indian accused of murdering a white rancher, and another Indian accused of murdering a Chinese. Now they wanted Ah Tai turned over to them.

"If you won't do this for us," Captain Charlie said, "you'll have an Indian massacre, and your whole town will burn."

The Whites, outnumbered by Indians, watched the formal inquest carefully. Ah Tai testified that the torso looked to him like mutton. A Frank Hanson testified that Ah Tai had wanted Hanson to defend him, if necessary. He also said Ah Tai had confessed to killing Poker Tom. Another witness said Ah Tai had also confessed to him.

But the Indians waited while the case went to a preliminary hearing. Ah Tai had engaged two men to defend him — neither one, of course, Frank Hanson. The defendant was discharged for insufficient evidence.

"You're free to go," one of his counsel told Ah Tai.

The frightened man grabbed his counsel's arms with such force that the imprints lasted several days.

"I need a guard," he pleaded. "I"ll pay five dollars a day."

Indians swarmed in when the courtroom doors opened. The justice of the peace begged them to not commit a crime in the courtroom. Indians pried Ah Tai loose from the death grip on his counsel and dragged him outside. They threw sand in his mouth to stifle his screams.

Ah Tai, a small man, wore a long queue which he sometime let hang to the ground. The Indians dismembered him as Poker Tom had been dismembered. They scattered the parts of his body. When they lopped off his head, an Indian grabbed the queue and swung it around his own head, as if competing in some ancient Scottish game. It flew far away into the sagebrush.

The Nevada Indians left immediately. The local Indians hid out for days. By then the county physician had the body parts gathered and buried.

Several months later, dogs belonging to George Day dragged into town a long black, braided queue attached to a piece of scalp. Day slung it over a rafter in his barn, where it attracted much attention.

Later, the queue — with attached scalp lock — was donated to a museum in the Fairmont Hotel in San Francisco. Many years after that, the sheriff's daughter — an eyewitness to the execution and dismemberment — learned that the museum had been moved and the queue and scalp lock could no longer be found.

"Wherever it is, may it rest in peace," she wrote.

Suggested reading: Ella Cody Cain, *The Story of Early Mono County* (San Francisco: Fearon Publishers, 1961).

THEY NEVER DID AMOUNT TO MUCH

On May 14, 1892, toward the end of the forty-year period of stage robberies in the West, two men held up the stage that ran from Shasta, California, to Redding. It probably would have drawn little interest if the robbers had not killed one of the most popular men in the region. That stage carried forty thousand dollars in gold from the Trinity Mines. Amos (Buck) Montgomery, Wells Fargo shotgun messenger, was riding guard.

It was near midnight as driver Johnny Boyce rounded a curve in the Middle Creek Road approaching Blue Cut. George Suhr, a blacksmith from French Gulch, sat beside him. Montgomery rode inside, a sawed-off shotgun across his knees. Suddenly a shadowy figure of a man appeared, shouting for the stage to stop. Boyce pulled up his eight-horse team.

"Throw down the box," the bandit ordered.

As Boyce complied, Montgomery drew back the curtains and fired. The bandit, blood streaming from his face and neck, fired back, hitting both Boyce and Suhr. Then two shots rang out from a chaparral thicket on the other side of the road. Buck Montgomery fell over, mortally wounded with two bullets in his back.

In spite of his wounds, Boyce drove to a farmhouse several miles away and gave the alarm. Before dawn several men from Redding had joined the sheriff and his deputies in a thorough search.

Shortly after daybreak they found the wounded bandit trying to drink from a ditch. He said his name was Lee Howard and his partner was Tom Horn. The posse took him to the Redding jail. More men joined the search for the second robber.

Two days later the arrested man was identified by a miner as Charley Ruggles.

"I know you," the miner said. "Where's your brother, John?"

Ruggles confessed, but insisted that John had nothing to do with the holdup. Learning that John was an ex-convict, the Sheriff had his description posted all over northern California. A month passed before a constable in Woodland captured John after a short gun battle in that city.

John readily admitted his part in the holdup, including the killing of Montgomery. He joined his brother in the Redding jail.

John said he and Charley — fifteen years younger — had been mining in the area of the holdup without success, and they knew of the large gold shipments being made on the stage.. He said he had left his brother after the holdup, believing him near death, and had cached the gold. He refused, in spite of intense grilling, to reveal its location.

Plans for the trial went ahead, and a well-known lawyer took the defense. Word leaked out to the community that the brothers would claim they had conspired with Montgomery to hold up the stage. Tempers flared at this insult to the integrity of the popular Montgomery, now dead. That some local women were carrying flowers and candy every day to handsome young Charley Ruggles did not help the situation.

Shortly after midnight on July 24, a few days before the trial was to start, a band of about seventy-five hooded men, reportedly including many of Redding's leading citizens, moved on the jail.

Jailer George Albro claimed he did not know the combination to the safe that held the jail keys. Twenty hooded men carried the safe out to the street, where it was blown open and the keys removed.

Charles Ruggles was dragged out first. Then the men told Albro to open up John's cell. Wielding a table leg, John came out fighting.

"Shoot him down," some shouted.

But they handcuffed him, put a hood over his head, and then locked jailer Albro in the cell.

John pleaded with the mob. "Don't hang Charley," he begged. "Save him for the trial and I'll tell you where the gold is hidden."

But the mob was more interested in Charley's neck than in Wells Fargo's treasure. "You're both coming with us," they said. "We don't care about the gold."

Working fast, they tied nooses around the necks of the doomed men. They used a windlass to hoist the twisting, choking victims up to a pipe running between two cottonwood trees.

Sixty-nine years later A. L. Paulson, who was seventeen years old at the time, reflected on the attitude of the Redding citizens:

"My mother's washerwoman, Mrs. Dunlap, was an aunt of the Ruggles boys," Paulson said. "She told my mother at the time: 'Well they never did amount to much.'"

As far as we know, no one ever found the gold.

Suggested reading: Eugene B. Block, *Great Stagecoach Robbers of the West* (Garden City: Doubleday & Company, 1962).

BRUTAL JUSTICE FOR A BRUTAL MAN

Cecilio Lucero wanted terribly to join the Vicente Silva gang, which had terrorized Las Vegas, New Mexico, for years. The gang was breaking up, but Cecilio begged Silva to let him show what he could do. Silva finally sent him to Colorado to see if he could steal sheep.

Cecilio returned in two months with a fifteen-year-old wife, Amadita, but no sheep.

"Where are the sheep?" Silva asked.

"There weren't many, and I had to sell them cheap to buy a horse and saddle for my wife."

"I saw her. She's a pretty little one."

Cecilio, tall and handsome, had had no trouble enticing Amadita to the altar. She had never been to school, and she yearned to escape poverty. Cecilio's promise of a three-bedroom house was a message from heaven.

"How did you get the sheep?" continued Silva.

"I tricked the boy herding them. I said his mother was dying and they sent me to care for them while he rode home. It was easy."

"Why didn't you tell that to someone who had more sheep?"

"They were all too wise, Señor."

"And you are too stupid. You should have killed the wise ones and got a bigger flock. We are not petty thieves, *Mister* Lucero. If you go out on a job again, let nothing stop you from making the most of it."

Silva's scolding rang in Cecilio's ears as he rode away. The *Mister* was a clear threat.

The next winter Amadita had a baby girl. Cecilio brought a midwife into their rude one-room hut, and paid her a dollar for her work. He paid another dollar for the baptismal party Amadita wanted.

In May, 1893, Cecilio, still determined to show Silva what he could do, got his chance. His cousin, Benigno Martinez, had a sheep camp near Vegoso. Benigno suspected his cousin Cecilio was involved with the Silva gang, but he employed him, thinking regular work would reform the young man. But Cecilio drove some of the sheep to Watrous and sold them. He told himself that if Benigno complained he would kill him.

Benigno did complain, and Cecilio shot him in the head. Then he turned and killed Juan Gallegos, his cousin's herder. Now he would make a name for himself and show Silva what he could do!

He found rocks and crushed the heads of the two men. Then he fastened each body to a burro, tied tin cans to the burros' tails, and drove them from the corral. Cecilio laughed as the animals galloped away, dragging their ghoulish burdens over the dry New Mexico plain.

When blood-drenched Cecilio got home, he told Amadita that he had butchered a steer.

By nightfall the next day the blood-curdling crime was being reported in newspapers across the territory. Cecilio went to one of Silva's hideouts, expecting to find the bandit *jefe* suitably impressed. But just five days before, Silva had been shot to death by four members of his gang. They had seen him kill his own wife, accusing her of disloyalty, and that was too much, even for them.

Cecilio went to his father's home and asked for help in escaping from the authorities. But Manuel Lucero had other ideas.

"I'll help you the only way I know how," he said. "I'll hire a lawyer to defend you, but first I must take you in so you can be tried in a court."

"But they'll hang me. You are my father!"

"That's a cross I'll bear until I die."

At the preliminary examination the hundreds of citizens who had come to town learned that the evidence was all circumstantial; no witness had seen the double killing. Legal maneuvering could save this man from hanging, or, even worse, result in an acquittal! A low gutteral roar could be heard from the crowd as it moved, as one man, toward Cecilio.

The magistrate hurriedly postponed the hearing. It was never completed.

At nine o'clock the next evening about a thousand armed men stormed the jail and forced Cecilio's cell open. They dragged him into the street and hanged him on a telegraph pole.

Cecilio struggled as he was hoisted upward. He got one foot on the pole and temporarily relieved the strain on his neck. But another jerk on the rope made him dangle in the air again.

Ten minutes passed. "He's still alive," someone shouted.

"Let him die twice. He killed two men."

The brutal crime had been avenged by a brutal substitute for justice.

Suggested reading: Mitchell Sena, "Third Rate Henchman of a First Rate Terror," in *True West,* Feb. 1970.

IMPATIENT CITIZENS

When Sheriff W. C. Ricker of Natrona County, Wyoming, reached the Charles Woodward ranch with his deputies, they put their horses in the barn and waited at the house. It was January 2, 1902, and Ricker had a warrant for Woodward for his escape from jail three nights before. The sheriff had been holding Woodward for trial on a grand larceny charge, but the prisoner, along with several other inmates, escaped by cutting a window bar.

Woodward recognized the horses when he rode up to his barn. He knew a posse waited somewhere near.

"I think I heard a noise down by the barn," Ricker told his men, as they waited in the house. "I'll go down for a look."

Woodward waited until Ricker was ten feet from the barn door before he shot. Then he struck the dying officer in the face with his six-shooter and robbed him of his gun, cartridge belt, and money. He jumped on one of the deputies' horses and escaped.

About ten days later, Woodward found work on a Laurel, Montana, ranch under a different name. The rancher recognized him, but promised to protect him. As soon as the rancher got assurance from Casper, Wyoming, that he would receive a reward if he captured Woodward, he turned the wanted man over to the authorities.

The Wyoming district court was in session, so Woodward got an early trial. Found guilty of murder, he was sentenced to hang on March 28.

A few minutes after midnight on the day of trial, twenty-four masked men knocked on the door of the sheriff's office, saying they had a prisoner to put in the jail. They overpowered the sheriff when he came to the door, and got the keys.

"You damn fools," the sheriff said. "He's already been sentenced to death. Let us hang him legally."

"We heard the supreme court gave him a new trial."

"They didn't. They just gave him a stay for a few days so they can decide his motion for a new trial. They'll never grant it."

"We ain't taking chances."

The vigilantes bound and gagged the sheriff and moved to Woodward's cell. The prisoner wore only a night shirt. When the masked men started taking him out, he begged them to let him get dressed.

"You ain't gonna freeze where you're going."

Woodward had to walk through sixty feet of snow in a bitterly cold wind to reach the gallows. The trembling man cried out when they put the rope around his neck.

"Boys, let me kneel down and pray for you! I want to pray for all of you. Tell my dear little wife that I love her dearly. Won't you tell her that, boys?"

They drew the noose up tighter around his neck.

"Don't choke me, boys. For God's sake, you are choking me. O, God, have mercy on me! Have mercy on my soul, and I pray for my blessed little wife. Don't choke me to death, boys! You are choking me."

With the rope tightly drawn, they tried to lift Woodward up on the trap door. He jumped off before they could pull the lever. Then several of the masked men grabbed him and threw him back on to the gallows. As his body slid back down, it convulsed and then twitched nervously, dangling in the air. Two men ran down the steps, grabbed Woodward's feet, and gave them several hard jerks.

They all stood back and watched the writhing form. Loud gurgling, which some later described as a sickening human sound, could be heard. Everyone was silent as the gurgling sounds grew fainter and fainter and Woodward slowly choked to death.

Someone stepped forward and pinned a card to Woodward's nightshirt:

> Process of law is a little slow,
> So this is the road you'll have to go.
> Murderers and thieves, Beware!

PEOPLE'S VERDICT

The coroner's jury said Woodward died by being hanged by unknown men. The governor ordered the prosecuting attorney to investigate and vigorously prosecute for debauching the state's fair name.

Like most of the citizens of Natrona County, the prosecutor thought the vigilance committee had done a good job. There was no investigation.

Suggested reading: Alfred J. Mokler, *History of Natrona County Wyoming* (Glendale: The Arthur H. Clark Co., 1923).

62

ORDERING INFORMATION

True Tales of the Old West
is projected for 40 volumes.

For Titles in Print —
Ask at your bookstore
or write:

PIONEER PRESS
P. O. Box 216
Carson City, NV 89702-0216
(775) 888-9867
FAX (775) 888-0908

Other titles in progress include:

Pioneer Children	Frontier Courts & Lawyers
Old West Riverboaters	Frontier Artists
Army Women	Californios
Western Duelists	Early West Explorers
Government Leaders	Homesteaders
Early Lumbermen	Old West Merchants
Frontier Militiamen	Scientists & Engineers
Preachers & Spirit Guides	Frontier Teachers
Teamsters & Packers	Visitors to the Frontier
Doctors & Healers	Storms & Floods
Mysteries & Ghosts	Wild Animals